TITANIC

TITANIC

Build Your Own *Titanic*
Die *Titanic* zum Selberbauen
Le *Titanic* à monter soi-même

TASCHEN

The *Titanic* – a Ship of Superlatives

The story of the *Titanic* began when Mr and Mrs Ismay were invited to dinner by Lord and Lady Pirrie at their London residence. Ismay was the director of one of Britain's biggest steamship companies, the White Star Line. Lord Pirrie was chairman of the board of directors of Harland & Wolff in Belfast, where all the ships of the White Star Line were built. After dinner Ismay and Pirrie somehow got onto the topic of plans for the future. They wanted to build three big transatlantic liners, bigger than any of the ships they had built so far. These steamers were not intended to be the fastest but rather the most spacious and luxurious ships in the world.

Although plans for the third ship were soon postponed, the work on the first two, the *Olympic* and the *Titanic*, proceeded very swiftly. At first the plans for the two ships were absolutely identical. But after some experience with building the *Olympic* it was decided that a number of changes should be made to the *Titanic*, so that the second ship ended up with more transport capacity,

Die *Titanic* – ein Schiff der Superlative

Alles hatte begonnen, als Mr. und Mrs. Bruce Ismay mit Lord und Lady Pirrie in deren Londoner Stadthaus dinierten. Ismay war Direktor einer der größten Dampfschifffahrtsgesellschaften Englands, der White Star Line. Lord Pirrie war Aufsichtsratsvorsitzender von Harland & Wolff in Belfast, wo die White Star Line alle ihre Schiffe bauen ließ. Nach dem Dinner begannen Ismay und Pirrie fast nebenbei Pläne zu schmieden. Sie wollten drei große Transatlantikliner bauen, größer als alle Schiffe, die sie bis dahin konstruiert hatten. Diese Dampfer sollten nicht die schnellsten, sondern die geräumigsten und luxuriösesten Schiffe der Welt werden.

Bald wurden die Pläne für das dritte Schiff aufgeschoben, doch die Arbeit an den beiden anderen, der *Olympic* und der *Titanic*, schritten schnell voran. Die Pläne für die beiden Schiffe waren zunächst grundsätzlich identisch. Erfahrungen beim Bau der *Olympic* ergaben aber für die *Titanic* einige Änderungen: So vergrößerte sich schließlich die Transportkapazität der *Titanic* auf 46 328 Bruttoregistertonnen, was sie zum

Le *Titanic* – un navire des superlatifs

Tout avait débuté lors d'un dîner offert, en leur demeure londonienne, par Monsieur et Madame Bruce Ismay à Lord Pirrie et à son épouse. Ismay dirigeait la White Star Line, une des plus grandes compagnies de navigation à vapeur d'Angleterre. Lord Pirrie, lui, présidait le conseil d'administration de l'entreprise Harland & Wolff, à Belfast, où la White Star Line faisait construire tous ses navires. Après le dîner, Ismay et Pirrie commencèrent à imaginer des plans pour le futur : ils voulaient construire trois gros transatlantiques, plus grands que tous les bateaux qu'ils avaient bâtis jusque-là. Non pas les plus rapides, mais plutôt les plus gigantesques, les plus luxueux des navires à vapeur.

On repoussa bientôt le projet d'un troisième navire, mais l'élaboration des deux autres, l'*Olympic* et le *Titanic*, avançait à grands pas. Au départ, les plans des deux bateaux reposaient sur les mêmes principes. Toutefois, en construisant l'*Olympic*, on décida d'apporter quelques modifications au *Titanic*. Sa capacité de transport de 46 328 tonneaux en faisait alors le plus grand navire

The White Star Line's New Triple-screw Steamers "OLYMPIC" ☆ "TITANIC"

Page 2: The Titanic *in Southampton dock before her maiden voyage, 1912.*

Seite 2: Die Titanic *im Dock von Southampton vor ihrer Jungfernfahrt, 1912.*

Page 2: Le Titanic *en cale sèche à Southampton avant son voyage inaugural, 1912.*

Photo: akg-images

This highly popular illustration shows the ship compared with tall buildings. The impression it gave was that the illustrator had searched the whole world for a construction of comparable height — but in vain.

Eine sehr beliebte Darstellung zeigt das Schiff im Vergleich mit hohen Bauwerken. Vergeblich, so schien es, hatte der Zeichner die Welt durchforscht, um etwas ähnlich Hohes zu finden.

Une illustration très populaire montre le navire comparé à divers édifices. Le dessinateur semble avoir cherché en vain une construction aussi élevée.

Illustration: Ralph White/Corbis

The Titanic *departing Queenstown harbour, Ireland, on 11 April 1912.*

Die Titanic *beim Auslaufen aus dem Hafen von Queenstown, Irland, am 11. April 1912.*

Le Titanic *quittant le port irlandais de Queenstown, le 11 avril 1912.*

Photo: akg-images/
Universal Images Group

i.e. 46,328 gross register tonnage, making her the largest ship in the world. With a bulk of 105 feet from keel to bridge and an overall length of 883 feet, she was about two and a half times as long as a football field, and her width of 92 feet made her wider than the length of a tennis court. Her walls jutted out 69 feet above water level, i.e. as high as a seven-storey building.

The enormous size of the *Titanic* meant that the press agency of the White Star Line had to show a great deal of imagination in their advertising campaign. One advertisement was particularly popular: it showed an open cross section of the steamer, deck upon deck, each one more magnificent and more sumptuously furnished than the other, thus proving the claim that the *Titanic* was the most luxurious ship in the world. The state rooms and first-class cabins were designed in the florid style of the Belle Époque. Numerous entertainment facilities were created by the designers. On the first floor of this large floating luxury hotel there was a Turkish bath. Together with several gymnasiums as well as a swimming pool and a squash court, it provided opportunities for physical exercise. Then there were a number of salons, a dining room, an à la carte restaurant, a

größten Schiff der Welt machte. Ihr Rumpf maß vom Kiel bis zur Kommandobrücke 32 m; das Schiff war 269 m lang, was dem Zweieinhalbfachen eines Fußballplatzes entspricht, und 28 m breit (breiter, als ein Tennisplatz lang ist). Die Bordwände ragten 21 m hoch über die Wasserlinie: so hoch wie ein siebenstöckiges Haus.

Die enorme Größe der *Titanic* stellte hohe Anforderungen an den Einfallsreichtum der White Star Line-Presseagenten. Eine beliebte Reklame war die Aufrisszeichnung des Querschnitts: Deck folgte auf Deck, eines prunkvoller und glänzender ausgestattet als das andere – wie es dem Anspruch der *Titanic* als dem luxuriösesten Schiff der Welt entsprach. Die Kabinen und Räume der ersten Klasse wurden im überladenen Stil der Belle Époque eingerichtet. Für die Unterhaltung der Gäste sorgten die Erbauer auf vielfältige Weise. Das türkische Bad im ersten Stock des siebenstöckigen schwimmenden Palasthotels diente neben zahlreichen Gymnastik- und Fitnessräumen, einem Schwimmbad und einem Squashplatz dem körperlichen Ausgleich der Passagiere. Wer sich in den Empfangshallen, im Speisesaal, im À-la-carte-Restaurant, im Rauchsalon, an der Bar und im Palmengarten nicht genügend amüsierte, konnte in

du monde. Le paquebot avait une longueur de 269 mètres, soit deux fois et demie la longueur d'un terrain de football, pour une largeur de 28 mètres – plus que la longueur d'un court de tennis. De la quille à la passerelle de commandement, la coque mesurait 32 mètres de hauteur, dont 21 mètres au-dessus de la ligne de flottaison – l'équivalent d'un bâtiment de sept étages.

Les gigantesques dimensions du *Titanic* exigèrent beaucoup d'imagination de la part des agents de presse de la White Star Line. Une publicité représentait un plan en coupe verticale du navire où se succédaient des ponts tous plus fastueux les uns que les autres, preuve que le *Titanic* était bien le paquebot le plus luxueux du monde. On aménagea les cabines et les salles de première classe de manière assez chargée, en style Belle Époque. Les possibilités de divertissement étaient nombreuses : au premier étage, on trouvait un bain turc, tandis que de nombreuses salles de gymnastique et de culture physique, une piscine et un court de squash assuraient la bonne forme physique des passagers. S'y ajoutaient des salles de réception, une salle à manger de plus de cinq cents places, un restaurant à la carte, un fumoir, un bar

Lifeboats on the promenade deck
of the Titanic, 1912.

Rettungsboote auf dem Promenadendeck
der Titanic, 1912.

Canots de sauvetage sur le pont promenade
de la Titanic, 1912.

smoking room, a bar and a palm garden. And if this was still not enough, you could always withdraw to the Café de Paris.

Praised as "unsinkable", the *Titanic* was launched from the Harland & Wolff dock in Belfast on 31 May 1911. She was called "unsinkable" because of a special construction that featured a double hull and six water-tight decks (decks A–G). These were separated from one another by 16 watertight bulkheads that ran verti-cally through the ship, although they did not in fact reach far enough to the top. The first two and the last five bulkheads went only as far as deck E. Nevertheless, it meant that the steamer could still have floated with two flooded compartments. And since nobody was able to imagine anything worse than a collision during which two compartments would be flooded, it was generally agreed that the *Titanic* was quite safe.

However, she would only have been completely safe if the bulkheads had been sealed by a subdivision deck at the top or, alternatively, if all the bulkheads had reached right up to the top deck. Instead, they ended on the second floor so that, after the accident, the water gushed from one compartment to another until it pressed down the bows. Nobody suspected these dan-gers when the ship was launched on her maiden voyage.

On 10 April the *Titanic* left Southampton for Cher-bourg. The captain in command, Edward J. Smith, was said to be the best-paid and most respected captain on all the seas.

The Last Hours and the Sinking of the *Titanic*

On 14 April 1912, after an undisturbed three-day journey, the *Titanic* approached the shore of Newfound-land at a speed of about 22 knots. She was running along the southern steamer route, which had been internatio-nally recognized as being less dangerous with regard to

das Café de Paris ausweichen.

Die als „unsinkbar" gepriesene *Titanic* lief am 31. Mai 1911 auf dem Dock von Harland & Wolff in Belfast vom Stapel. Das Etikett „unsinkbar" erhielt das Schiff durch eine besondere Konstruktion: Die *Titanic* hatte einen doppelten Boden und war in sechs wasserdichte Decks unterteilt (Deck A–G); diese wurden von 16 wasserdichten Schotten abgetrennt, die vertikal durch das Schiff führten. Sie reichten aber nicht weit genug hinauf. Die ersten beiden und die letzten fünf Schotten reichten nur bis zum E-Deck. Dennoch konnte der Dampfer selbst mit zwei gefluteten Abteilungen noch schwimmen, und da sich niemand Schlimmeres vorzu-stellen vermochte als einen Zusammenstoß, bei dem zwei Abteilungen voll Wasser laufen würden, galt die *Titanic* als sehr sicher.

Doch wirklich sicher wäre sie nur in dem Fall gewe-sen, wenn die Schotten entweder oben durch ein Schot-tendeck verschlossen gewesen wären oder wenn alle Schotten bis zum Oberdeck hinaufgereicht hätten. Sie endeten aber im 2. Stock, und so schwappte das Wasser nach dem Unfall von Abteilung zu Abteilung und drück-te den Bug in die Tiefe. Von solchen Gefahren ahnte niemand etwas, als das Schiff zu seiner Jungfernfahrt aufbrach: Am 10. April 1912 verließ die *Titanic* South-ampton in Richtung Cherbourg. Kapitän Edward J. Smith, der den Dampfer kommandierte, galt als der höchstbezahlte und meist bewunderte Kapitän aller Meere.

Die letzten Stunden und der Untergang der *Titanic*

Nach dreitägiger planmäßiger Fahrt mit einer Ge-schwindigkeit von ca. 22 Knoten näherte sich die *Tita-nic* am 14. April 1912 den Neufundlandbänken. Obwohl sie auf dem international vereinbarten südlichen Dampfertrack lief, auf dem die Eis- und Nebelgefahr

et même une palmeraie. Et si on n'y trouvait pas son bonheur, on pouvait toujours passer au Café de Paris.

Le *Titanic* quitta la cale du dock de l'entreprise Harland & Wolff le 31 mai 1911 à Belfast. Un détail de construction lui valait d'être réputé insubmersible : le navire possédait un double fond et était divisé en six ponts étanches (ponts A–G), séparés par seize cloisons étanches qui traversaient le navire de bas en haut. Les deux premières comme les cinq dernières cloisons, toutefois, n'atteignaient que le pont E, mais cela signi-fiait que le navire pouvait encore flotter avec deux com-partiments inondés. On ne pouvait imaginer pire acci-dent, et le *Titanic* passait donc pour être très sûr.

Il l'aurait été totalement si les cloisons étanches avaient été fermées au sommet par un pont de cloison, ou avaient toutes atteint le pont supérieur. Malheureu-sement, elles s'arrêtaient au deuxième étage, et après la collision, l'eau déborda d'une division à l'autre, faisant basculer la proue vers les profondeurs. Mais personne ne soupçonnait ces dangers quand le *Titanic* entreprit sa croisière inaugurale, le 10 avril 1912, quittant South-ampton pour Cherbourg. Le capitaine Edward J. Smith, qui était alors aux commandes, passait pour être le mieux rémunéré et le plus respecté du monde entier.

Les dernières heures et le naufrage du *Titanic*

Le 14 avril 1912, après trois jours de croisière con-formes aux prévisions, le *Titanic* s'approcha à une vitesse de 22 nœuds environ des hauts-fonds de Terre-Neuve. Bien qu'il suivît la route sud, qui avait été déterminée au niveau international pour les navires à vapeur et dont on estimait les dangers dus au brouillard et aux glaces inférieurs à ceux de la route nord, pourtant plus courte, la catastrophe se produisit. Elle aurait pu être évitée : certes, la sécurité sur le bateau était insuffisante pour des raisons techniques, mais l'équipage avait manqué

fog and ice than the shorter, northern one. Nevertheless, the disaster happened, although it was by no means inevitable. In fact, it could have been averted if more attention had been paid to safety, both technically and also by the crew themselves, and if the captain had taken the right steps when he saw himself faced with a dangerous situation. On that day he had already had five ice warnings, which he chose to ignore. If he had taken these warnings seriously and moved his course further south, and if he had reduced speed at sunset, the *Titanic* would not have collided with the iceberg. But as there was excellent visibility and the sea was calm, he relied on the lookouts, without making any changes in speed or direction. Only two seamen were peering from the masthead into the clear, moonless night – and without binoculars! There was no second lookout post, neither in the bows nor at the two sides of the bridge, as would have been standard on any other ship. Neither had the *Titanic* been equipped with searchlights, which had been in use for quite a while in the British navy. This meant that the fate of the largest ship in the world was entirely dependent on no more than four eyes!

11.40 p.m.: The lookout post reported: "Iceberg ahead. Distance 500 yards." It would have been possible to see the iceberg with binoculars, and, according to one of the two seamen on duty, they would have been able to

geringer eingeschätzt wurde als auf der kürzeren, weiter nördlich gelegenen Route, kam es doch zu der – vermeidbaren – Katastrophe. Vermeidbar deshalb, weil das Schiff in puncto Sicherheit sowohl technisch als auch von der Besatzung her ungenügend gerüstet war und der Kapitän angesichts der Gefahr nicht angemessen handelte. Er hatte am 14. April fünf Eiswarnungen in den Wind geschlagen. Hätte er aufgrund der Warnungen den Kurs weiter südlich verlegt und mit Einbruch der Dunkelheit die Geschwindigkeit gedrosselt, wäre der Zusammenstoß mit dem Eisberg nicht erfolgt. Doch weil die Sicht klar und das Meer ruhig war, vertraute man dem Ausguck und behielt Kurs und Geschwindigkeit bei. Allerdings spähten nur zwei Matrosen vom Mastkorb aus in die klare, mondlose Nacht, und das auch noch ohne Fernglas! Kein weiterer Ausguck, weder am Bug noch an den Seiten der Kommandobrücke war, wie bei anderen Schiffen üblich, postiert worden. Außerdem besaß die *Titanic* keine Suchscheinwerfer, die schon längst zur Ausstattung britischer Kriegsschiffe gehörten. So war das Schicksal des größten Schiffes der Erde von nur vier Augen abhängig!

Um 23 Uhr 40 meldete der Ausguck: „Eisberg voraus. Abstand 500 m." Mit Fernglas hätte der Eisberg auf größere Entfernung erkannt werden können. Laut Aussage der beiden Matrosen sogar früh genug, um daran

d'attention, et le capitaine n'avait pas réagi comme la situation l'exigeait. Le 14 avril, il avait fait fi de cinq avertissements annonçant des icebergs. S'il avait changé de cap et choisi une route située plus au sud, s'il avait diminué la vitesse à la tombée de la nuit, il n'y aurait pas eu de collision. Mais comme la nuit était claire et la mer calme, on continua à faire confiance à la vigie, et on conserva le même cap et la même vitesse. Seuls deux marins scrutaient de la hune, sans jumelles, la nuit claire et sans lune. On n'avait posté aucune autre vigie, ni à la proue, ni sur la passerelle de commandement comme c'est l'usage sur les autres bateaux. De plus, le *Titanic* ne disposait pas des projecteurs de recherche dont les bateaux de guerre britanniques étaient équipés depuis longtemps. La destinée du plus grand paquebot du monde dépendait donc de deux paires d'yeux !

À 23 h 40, la vigie donna le signal suivant : « Iceberg droit devant à 500 mètres ! » Des jumelles auraient permis de repérer l'obstacle plus tôt. Selon les deux marins, assez tôt, même, pour pouvoir l'éviter. Le premier officier, qui remplaçait le capitaine sur la passerelle, donna les ordres que tout marin aurait donnés dans cette situation : gouvernail à bâbord, stopper les machines. Trop tard : la coque était déjà fendue. L'eau pénétra aussitôt dans les cloisonnements avant. Thomas Andrews, le constructeur du *Titanic*, qui se trouvait à bord,

Left: The second and third class decks of the Titanic.

Links: Die Decks der zweiten und dritten Klasse der Titanic.

À gauche : Les ponts de la deuxième et troisième classe de la Titanic.

Right: Edward John Smith, the captain of the Titanic.

Rechts: Edward John Smith, der Kapitän der Titanic.

À droite : Edward John Smith, le capitaine de la Titanic.

Photos: akg-images / Universal Images Group

The smart Café de Paris on the Titanic's deck B was designed in the style of a French street café and was particularly popular amongst the younger passengers in first class.

Das festliche Café de Paris auf dem B-Deck der Titanic *war im Stil eines französischen Straßencafés gestaltet und besonders bei den jüngeren Passagieren der ersten Klasse sehr beliebt.*

Le festif Café de Paris du pont B du Titanic *était aménagé dans le style d'un café-terrasse français et particulièrement prisé par les jeunes passagers de la première classe.*

Photo: akg-images/ Universal Images Group

make it out in good time so that the ship could have steered clear of it. The first officer, who was taking the captain's place on the bridge, gave orders that any seaman would have given in this situation: put helm to port quickly, stop engines. Too late. The hull had already been slit open. Immediately the front bulkheads were filled with water. Thomas Andrew, the designing engineer who was on the *Titanic* at the time, quickly worked out that the ship could not be saved and was going to sink.

12.05 a.m.: The first passengers were woken up. Most of them had not noticed the disaster at this stage.

12.15 a.m.: The first alarm signal.

The *Titanic* had about 20 lifeboats with enough space for 1178 people, although there were 2224 passengers on board. The first lifeboat was lowered at 12.45 a.m. and was soon followed by a second and third boat. They could have seated 240 people, but there were only 63 in them. Many passengers still believed that the ship could not possibly sink, while others were afraid of climbing into the lifeboats.

1.40 a.m.: The last distress signal was fired.

vorbeizukommen. Der erste Offizier, der in Vertretung des Kapitäns auf der Brücke stand, gab Kommandos, die jeder Seemann in dieser Situation gegeben hätte: Ruder hart Backbord, Maschinen voll zurück. Zu spät. Der Rumpf war bereits aufgeschlitzt. Sofort drang Wasser in die vorderen Schotten. Die nun vom Konstrukteur der *Titanic*, Thomas Andrews, der sich auf dem Schiff befand, sofort angestellten Berechnungen ergaben, dass das Schiff nicht mehr zu retten war und sinken musste.

Um 0 Uhr 5 wurden die ersten Passagiere geweckt. Die meisten hatten das Unglück noch gar nicht bemerkt.

0 Uhr 15: Erster Notruf.

Die *Titanic* besaß rund 20 Rettungsboote mit Platz für rund 1178 Personen. Es befanden sich aber 2224 Menschen an Bord. 0 Uhr 45 wurde das erste Boot gefiert, gleich darauf ein zweites und drittes. Sie hätten zusammen 240 Menschen aufnehmen können, aber es saßen nur 63 darin. Für viele Passagiere war das Sinken des Schiffes noch immer undenkbar, andere hatten Angst, in ein Boot zu steigen.

1 Uhr 40: Die letzte Notrakete wurde abgefeuert.

présenta alors des calculs qui prouvaient qu'il n'était plus possible de sauver le bateau et qu'il devait donc sombrer.

À 0 h 05, on réveilla les premiers passagers. La plupart d'entre eux ne s'étaient pas encore rendu compte de la situation.

À 0 h 15 retentit le premier signal de détresse.

Le *Titanic* possédait environ 20 canots de sauvetage pouvant accueillir quelque 1 178 personnes. Or, il y avait 2 224 personnes à bord. À 0 h 45, on mit le premier canot à l'eau, suivi d'un deuxième puis d'un troisième. Ils auraient pu transporter 240 personnes, mais seulement 63 passagers y trouvèrent place. Nombre d'entre eux ne pouvaient toujours pas croire au naufrage, d'autres craignaient de monter dans un canot.

À 1 h 40, on lança la dernière fusée de détresse. À 2 h 05, on mit le dernier canot de sauvetage à l'eau.

À 2 h 10 fut envoyé le dernier message radio.

À 2 h 15, le *Titanic* se dressait presque à la verticale de sa proue.

À 2 h 20, il avait sombré.

À 16 h 10, le *Carpathia*, qui s'était rendu au plus vite

The Grand Staircase in first class was the Titanic's *most spectacular architectural feature. The banisters were made of wrought iron with a bronze décor of flowers and leaves.*

Die große Treppe in der ersten Klasse war Titanic. *Das Geländer bestand aus Eisen, verziert mit Bronze-Einlagen in Form von Blättern und Blumen.*

Le grand escalier de la première classe était le joyau du Titanic. *La rampe en fer forgé était incrustée de feuilles et de fleurs en bronze.*

Photo: akg-images/ Universal Images Group

2.05 a.m.: The last lifeboat was lowered into the water.

2.10 a.m.: Last radio message.

2.15 a. m.: The *Titanic* was standing almost vertically on her bow.

2.20 a.m.: The *Titanic* had sunk.

4.10 a.m.: The *Carpathia*, which had hurried to the scene of the disaster at full speed, collected the 711 surviving passengers; 1513 people could no longer be saved. The managing director of the White Star Line, Bruce J. Ismay, who was among the survivors, remained a social outcast for the rest of his life.

Mysteries and Myths Surrounding the *Titanic*

So much for the facts. All witnesses agreed that the *Titanic* had collided with an iceberg at 11.40 p.m. and sunk at 2.20 a.m. What happened in the meantime, though, is largely shrouded in mystery, and the various statements and estimates are often totally contradictory. This is because the witnesses were too much under the influence of the disaster to be able to give a realistic account of the event.

2 Uhr 05: Das letzte Rettungsboot wurde zu Wasser gelassen.

2 Uhr 10: letzter Funkspruch.

2 Uhr 15: Die *Titanic* stand fast senkrecht auf dem Bug.

Um 2 Uhr 20 war sie versunken.

Um 4 Uhr 10 nahm die *Carpathia*, die mit Volldampf an die Unglücksstelle geeilt war, alle 711 Überlebenden auf. Für 1513 Menschen gab es keine Rettung mehr. Der Generaldirektor der White Star Line, J. Bruce Ismay, gehörte zu den Überlebenden: Er blieb sein ganzes Leben lang gesellschaftlich geächtet.

Ungelöste Rätsel und Mythen um die *Titanic*

Soweit die Tatsachen. Daneben ist jedoch vieles geheimnisvoll geblieben. Alle Zeugen sind sich einig, dass die *Titanic* um 23 Uhr 40 auf den Eisberg auflief und um 2 Uhr 20 sank. Aber über alles, was dazwischen passierte, gehen die Schätzungen und Aussagen diametral auseinander. Die Zeugen standen viel zu sehr unter dem Einfluss der Katastrophe, als dass ihre Aussagen realistisch hätten sein können.

sur le lieu du sinistre, prit à son bord 711 survivants. Le naufrage avait fait 1 513 victimes. Bruce J. Ismay, le directeur de la White Star Line, faisait partie des rescapés. Il fut banni par la société jusqu'à la fin de ses jours.

Énigmes et création d'un mythe autour du *Titanic*

Voilà pour les faits. Toutefois, beaucoup de points sont demeurés obscurs. Tous les témoins affirment que le *Titanic* a heurté l'iceberg à 23 h 40 et qu'il a sombré à 2 h 20. Mais les estimations et les affirmations sur tout ce qui s'est passé entre-temps sont souvent complètement contradictoires : le choc causé par la catastrophe fut trop grand pour permettre aux témoins des dépositions réalistes.

Les affirmations contradictoires au sujet de ce que jouait l'orchestre quand le bateau coula en fournissent un exemple. Beaucoup de rescapés ont persisté à affirmer, toute leur vie, que l'orchestre jouait « Plus près de toi, mon Dieu ». Pour diverses raisons, les dépositions de l'opérateur radio semblent plus probables. Il se rappelait qu'on jouait l'hymne « Autumn ».

Left: The gymnasium on the Titanic: trainer and sports teacher Thomas W. McCawley (aged 36) on a rowing machine; in the background, electrical engineer William Parr on a mechanical camel (both men were drowned in the catastrophe).

Links: Fitnessraum auf der Titanic: Der Trainer und Sportlehrer Thomas W. McCawley (36 Jahre) auf einer Rudermaschi-

ne; im Hintergrund der Bordelektriker William Parr auf einem mechanischen Kamel (beide ertranken bei der Katastrophe).

À gauche : Salle de musculation du Titanic : l'entraîneur et professeur de sport W. McCawley (36 ans) sur un rameur ; au fond de la salle, l'électricien de bord William Parr sur un chameau mécanique (les deux hommes périrent noyés dans la catastrophe).

Right: Emancipated ladies could join the gentlemen in the gymnasium to test their muscles.

Rechts: Emanzipierte Damen konnten im Trainingraum bei den Herren ihre Muskeln testen.

À droite : Des dames émancipées mesurent leur force musculaire dans la salle de culture physique, sur le pont du navire.

Photos: akg-images/ Universal Images Group

One example of these contradictions is the tune that the band was playing when the ship was going down. Many of the survivors continued to insist for the rest of their lives that the band was playing "Nearer, my God, to Thee". But according to Harold Bride, the junior radio operator, they were playing a piece called "Autumn". There are a variety of reasons why his statements can be regarded as more reliable.

Similarly there used to be a legend that Ismay escaped from the ship disguised as a woman. This legend has long been disproved and turned out to be no more than the fabrication of a vengeful journalist.

Until the sinking of the *Titanic* there had been a firm belief in technology, progress and the omnipotence of science. This faith had been shaken to the core.

And yet, as Joseph Conrad pointed out in 1912, the disaster had been entirely predictable. He grimly commented that a 46,000-ton hotel with thin steel plates had been built to win the favour of a thousand wealthy people; that it was decorated in the style of the Pharaos and Louis XV just to please some ridiculous individuals who had more money in their pockets than they were able to spend; that this massive construction with 2000 people on board was hurled into the sea at the speed of 21 knots – and then it happened.

Nevertheless, a number of people had become wiser after the disaster: from 1912 onwards sea voyages were made safer. It was decided in national and international committees that all ships had to provide enough lifeboat accommodation for all passengers and that every ship could be contacted round the clock via a radio operator. An International Ice Guard was also established to warn ships of icebergs.

Ein Beispiel dafür sind die widersprüchlichen Behauptungen darüber, was die Band spielte, als das Schiff unterging. Viele Überlebende beharrten ihr ganzes Leben lang darauf, sie habe „Näher mein Gott zu dir" gespielt. Die Aussagen des Juniorfunkers Harold Bride scheinen aus verschiedenen Gründen realistischer. Er erinnerte sich, dass die Hymne „Autumn" gespielt wurde.

Ebenso ist die Legende längst dementiert, dass Ismay als Frau verkleidet dem sinkenden Schiff entkam. Die Behauptung entpuppte sich als Hirngespinst eines rachsüchtigen Journalisten.

Der Glaube der modernen Welt an die Technik, den Fortschritt und die Allmacht der Wissenschaft war nach dem Untergang der *Titanic* zutiefst erschüttert.

Dabei hätte sich die Katastrophe voraussehen lassen, meinte der Schriftsteller Joseph Conrad 1912 grimmig: „Man baut ein 46 000-Tonnen-Hotel aus dünnen Stahlplatten, um die Gunst von tausend reichen Leuten zu gewinnen; man dekoriert es im Stil der Pharaos und von Louis Quinze, um diesen albernen Individuen zu gefallen, die mehr Geld in der Tasche haben, als sie ausgeben können, und unter dem Beifall zweier Kontinente schleudert man diese Masse mit 2000 Menschen an Bord mit 21 Knoten übers Meer – dann passiert's."

Immerhin wurden einige durch die Katastrophe klüger: Noch 1912 wurde die Seefahrt sicherer gemacht. Es mussten nun auf den Schiffen für alle Passagiere Plätze in Rettungsbooten zur Verfügung stehen. Zu jeder Tages- und Nachtstunde musste auf jedem Schiff ein Funker erreichbar sein; eine „Internationale Eiswache" wurde eingerichtet, die die Schiffe vor Eisbergen warnen sollte.

De même, on a depuis longtemps démenti la rumeur selon laquelle Ismay se serait échappé du navire déguisé en femme. Cette affirmation s'avéra l'œuvre d'un journaliste assoiffé de vengeance.

La foi du monde moderne en la technique, le progrès et la toute-puissance de la science fut profondément ébranlée par le naufrage du *Titanic*. Et pourtant on aurait pu prévoir la catastrophe, affirma en 1912 l'écrivain Joseph Conrad, furieux : « On construit un hôtel de 46 000 tonneaux avec de minces plaques d'acier afin de se gagner les faveurs d'un millier de nantis ; on le décore selon le style des pharaons ou en Louis XV pour plaire à des individus ridicules, qui ont bien trop d'argent pour pouvoir le dépenser ; puis, sous les applaudissements de deux continents, on lance cette masse, avec 2 000 personnes à son bord, à la vitesse de 21 nœuds – et c'est alors qu'arrive la catastrophe. »

Certains, cependant, surent tirer les leçons du sinistre. Dès 1912, les normes de sécurité pour la navigation maritime furent rendues plus sévères. Les conseils nationaux et internationaux décidèrent ainsi que les canots de sauvetage devaient être en nombre suffisant pour recevoir tous les passagers. On devait pouvoir joindre un opérateur radio sur tous les bateaux, à toute heure du jour et de la nuit. Un système d'alerte international fut également mis en place pour prévenir les navires de la présence d'icebergs.

S *Sun deck;* A *upper promenade deck;*
B *promenade deck (glassed-in);* C *top deck;*
D *saloon deck;* E *main deck;* F *middle deck;*
G *lower deck, storage, coal, boilers,*
machine-room; **a)** *davits and lifeboats;*
b) *bilge;* **c)** *double hull*

S *Sonnendeck;* A *Oberes Promenadendeck;*
B *Promenadendeck mit Verglasung;*
C *Oberdeck;* D *Salondeck;* E *Hauptdeck;*
F *Mitteldeck;* G *Unterdeck, Ladung, Kohlenbun-*
ker, Kessel, Maschinen; **a)** *Welin-Davits mit*
Rettungsbooten; **b)** *Bilge;* **c)** *doppelter Boden*

S *Pont pour bains de soleil ;* A *pont promenade*
supérieur ; B *pont promenade véranda ;* C *pont*
supérieur ; D *pont-salon ;* E *pont principal ;*
F *pont moyen ;* G *premier point cargaison, soute*
à charbon, chaudière, machines ; **a)** *bossoirs*
Wellin avec canots de sauvetage ; **b)** *fond de cale ;*
c) *double fond.*

The Titanic *colliding with an iceberg,*
14 April 1912. From Le Petit Journal, *Paris,*
28 April 1912.

Die Titanic *bei der Kollision mit einem*
Eisberg, 14. April 1912. Aus Le Petit
Journal, *Paris, 28. April 1912.*

Le Titanic *entrant en collision avec un*
iceberg, 14 avril 1912. Le Petit Journal,
Paris, 28 avril 1912.

Illustrations: Universal Images Group/
Getty Images

New Light Thrown on the Sinking and the Discovery of the Missing Wreck

Until quite recently nobody had any clear idea about the sequence of events as they occurred during the disaster. At the time shipping companies were rather reluctant to disclose any information. This reluctance, together with the sensationalist attitude of the press and a lack of technical equipment, contributed to the formation of legends and a general mystification of the accident.

The absence of information also raised the hopes of numerous treasure-hunters. However, by the time the steamer lay approximately 13,000 feet below the sea, i.e. too low for divers to reach, everything seemed lost.

Aufklärung des Untergangs und Entdeckung des verschollenen Wracks

Bis vor kurzem konnte man sich kein klares Bild vom Ablauf der Katastrophe machen. Die undurchsichtige Informationspolitik der Reedereien, die Sensationslüsternheit der Presse, aber auch der Mangel an technischen Geräten trugen zu einer Legendenbildung und Mystifizierung des Unglücks bei.

Die Fehlinformationen ließen auch zahlreiche Schatzsucher Hoffnung schöpfen. Da jedoch der Dampfer in fast 4000 m Tiefe liegt, wo Taucharbeiten bis vor kurzem unmöglich waren, schien alles verloren.

Projekte und Versuche, das Wrack aufzuspüren, setzten 1963 ein. Doch die meisten Ideen scheiterten an

Explication du naufrage et découverte de l'épave engloutie

Jusqu'à ces dernières années, on n'avait guère d'informations sur le déroulement précis de la catastrophe. Les réticences des armateurs, combinées au sensationnalisme de la presse et au manque d'équipements techniques, contribuèrent à la naissance de quantité de légendes et d'idées erronées.

De nombreux chasseurs de trésors bâtirent de vains espoirs sur cette absence d'informations. Mais le navire se trouvant à 4 000 mètres de fond, profondeur à laquelle, il y a peu de temps encore, les travaux en plongée étaient impossibles, la cause semblait perdue.

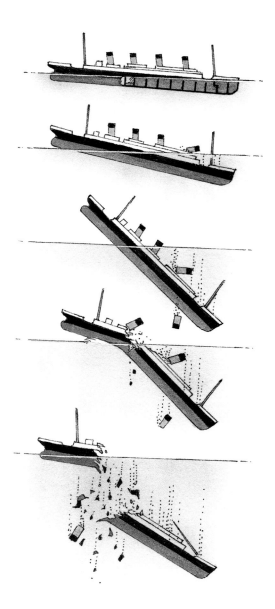

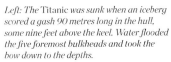

Left: The Titanic *was sunk when an iceberg scored a gash 90 metres long in the hull, some nine feet above the keel. Water flooded the five foremost bulkheads and took the bow down to the depths.*

Links: So sank die Titanic: *Der Eisberg fügte ihr drei Meter über dem Kiel einen 90 Meter langen, allerdings nicht durchgehenden Riss zu. Das Wasser schoss in die vorderen fünf Schotten und drückte den Bug in die Tiefe.*

À gauche : Voici comment le Titanic *a sombré : à trois mètres au-dessus de la quille, l'iceberg érafla le navire sur une longueur de 90 mètres, créant nombre d'enfoncements et de brèches. L'eau s'engouffra dans les cinq premiers compartiments, entraînant la proue vers les profondeurs.*

Illustration: Getty Images/ Dorling Kindersley

Right: Illustrated cross-section of the luxury liner Titanic *showing decks, storage areas etc. as well as probable points of impact with the iceberg below the waterline.*

Rechts: Querschnitt durch den Luxusdampfer Titanic, *der die verschiedenen Decks und Lagerbereiche sowie die vermutlichen Kollisionsstellen des Schiffes mit dem Eisberg unterhalb der Wasserlinie zeigt.*

À droite : Coupe transversale illustrée du luxueux transatlantique Titanic *montrant ponts, aires de stockage etc., ainsi que les points d'impact probables de l'iceberg sous la ligne de flottaison.*

Illustration: Time Life Pictures/ Getty Images

Left: The Titanic *in Queenstown (today Cobh) harbour, Ireland, her last port of call before the voyage across the Atlantic, 11 April 1912. Hawkers who had come on board illegally were obliged to leave the ship.*

Links: Letzter Halt der Titanic *im Hafen von Queenstown (heute Cobh), Irland, vor der Fahrt über den Atlantik, 11. April 1912. Händler, die illegal an Bord gekommen waren, mussten das Schiff verlassen.*

À gauche : Dernière escale du Titanic *dans le port de Queenstown (aujourd'hui Cobh), Irlande, le 11 avril 1912 avant la traversée de l'Atlantique. Des marchands montés à bord illégalement durent quitter le navire.*

Right: Captain John Edward Smith (very top) watches passengers boarding, Queenstown, Ireland, before the voyage across the Atlantic, 11 April 1912.

Rechts: Kapitän John Edward Smith (ganz oben) beobachtet die Ausschiffung von Passagieren auf eine Hafenfähre, Queenstown, Irland, vor der Fahrt über den Atlantik, 11. April 1912.

À droite : Le capitaine John Edward Smith (tout en haut) surveille le débarquement des passagers sur un ferry du port de Queenstown, Irlande, le 11 avril 1912 avant la traversée de l'Atlantique.

Photos: akg-images/
Universal Images Group

Since 1963 there have been a number of projects and attempts to retrieve the wreck, but most of them turned out to be unpracticable for both technical and financial reasons. In 1973 and in competition with others, the American marine biologist Robert Ballard began to take an interest in the question of how one might locate the wreck. In 1980 he succeeded in securing the support of the U.S. Navy for the joint development of an underwater searching system together with his institute; the navy was interested in a possible military application, while Ballard was thinking of the *Titanic*.

After five years of intensive searching the institute was successful: on the night of 1 September 1985 the wreck of the *Titanic* became visible on the screen. For four days two underwater cameras took 20,000 pictures of the ruins of the sunken luxury hotel. No bodies or bones could be made out, because they had already been dissolved completely by bacteria.

The cameras revealed that the area which was strewn with wreckage was about as large as 15 football fields. There were pieces of coal, suitcases, copper frying pans, silver plates, springs, chamber pots and wine

der technischen Undurchführbarkeit und dem Mangel an Geldgebern. 1973 begann sich der amerikanische Meeresbiologe Robert Ballard im Wettlauf mit anderen für die Frage zu interessieren, wie das Wrack gefunden werden könnte. 1980 gewann Ballard die amerikanische Marine für die Idee, gemeinsam mit seinem Institut ein Unterwassersuchsystem zu entwickeln; die Marine dachte dabei an eine militärische Verwendung. Ballard dachte an die *Titanic*.

Nach fünf Jahren intensiver Bemühungen war es endlich soweit: In der Nacht zum 1. September 1985 zeigte der Bildschirm des Systems das Wrack der *Titanic*. Vier Tage lang nahmen zwei Kameraschlitten 20 000 Bildern von den Resten des versunkenen Palasthotels auf. Leichen und Knochen konnten sie nicht ausmachen, denn die waren bereits von Bakterien völlig aufgelöst worden.

Die Kameras zeigten um das Wrack herum ein Trümmerfeld, so groß wie 15 Fußballplätze, mit Kohlenstücken, Koffern, Kupferpfannen, Silberplatten, Sprungfedern, Nachttöpfen und Weinflaschen, die sich sogar nach ihrer Form identifizieren ließen: Madeira, Portwein, Champagner und Bordeaux.

En 1963 débuta une série de projets et d'essais visant à retrouver l'épave, mais la plupart échouèrent pour des raisons techniques ou financières.

En 1973, le biologiste marin Robert Ballard se lança à son tour dans la compétition et commença à s'intéresser à la question des moyens nécessaires à la découverte de l'épave. En 1980, il réussit à persuader la marine américaine de collaborer avec son institut au développement d'un système de repérage sous-marin. La marine envisageait une utilisation à des fins militaires ; Ballard, de son côté, pensait au *Titanic*.

Après cinq années d'efforts intensifs, l'heure de la victoire sonna enfin : dans la nuit du 1er septembre 1985, l'épave du *Titanic* apparut sur les écrans. Pendant quatre jours, deux caméras sous-marines prirent vingt mille photos des restes du palace englouti. Aucun reste humain – cadavres ou ossements – ne put être mis en évidence : les bactéries avaient fait leur œuvre. Autour de l'épave, les caméras montrèrent un amas de décombres aussi vaste que quinze terrains de football. On y reconnaissait du charbon, des valises, des poêles en cuivre, des plateaux d'argent, des ressorts de matelas, des pots de chambre et des bouteilles de vin qu'on pou-

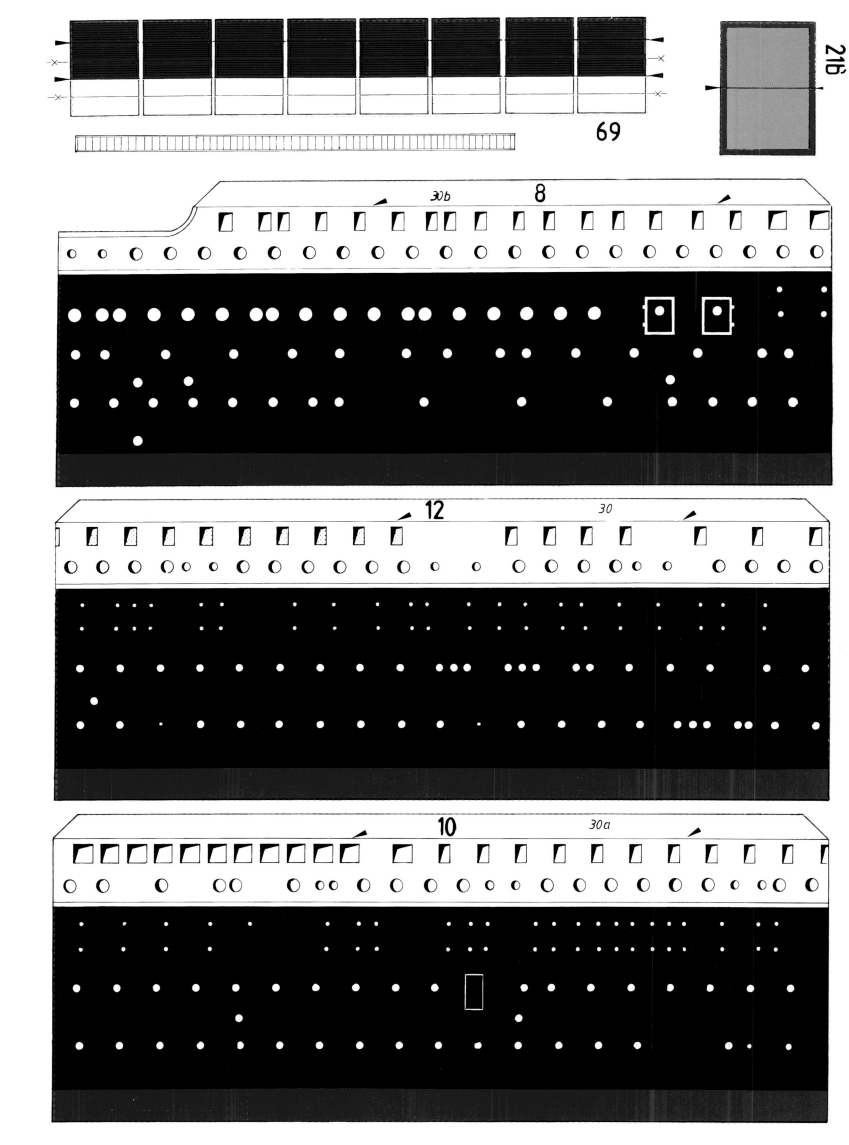

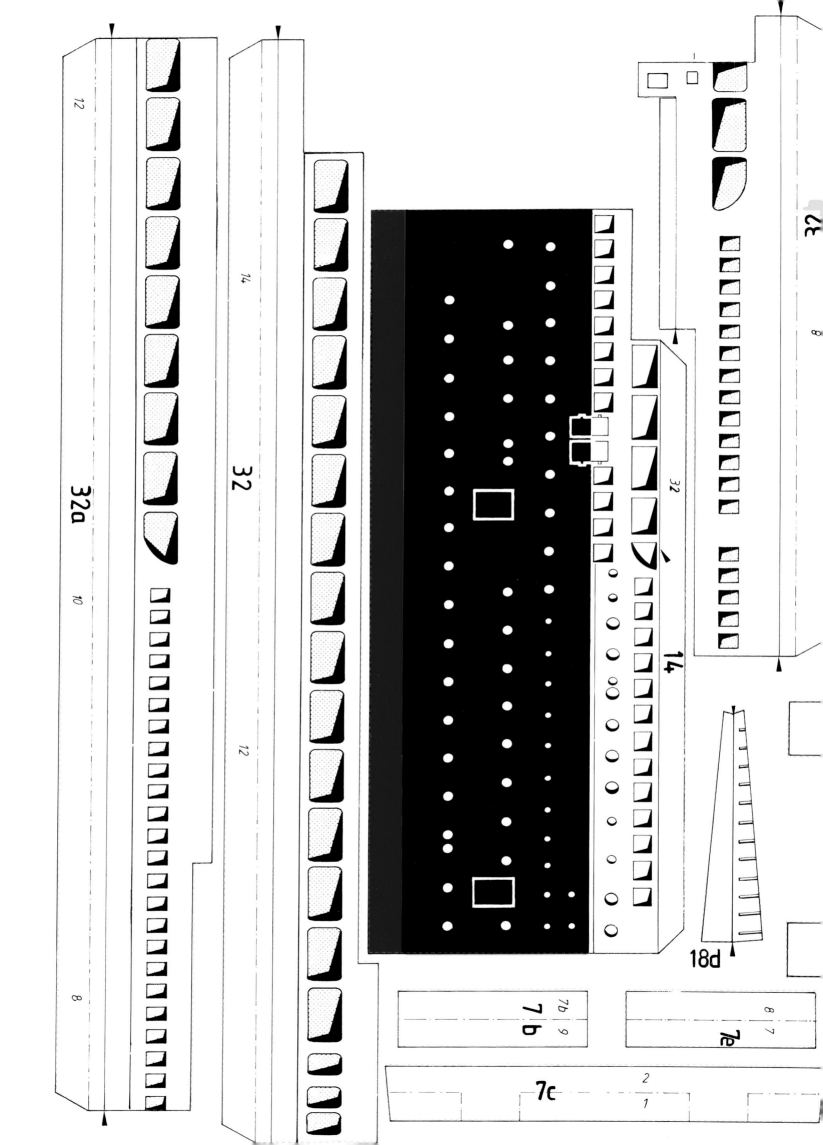

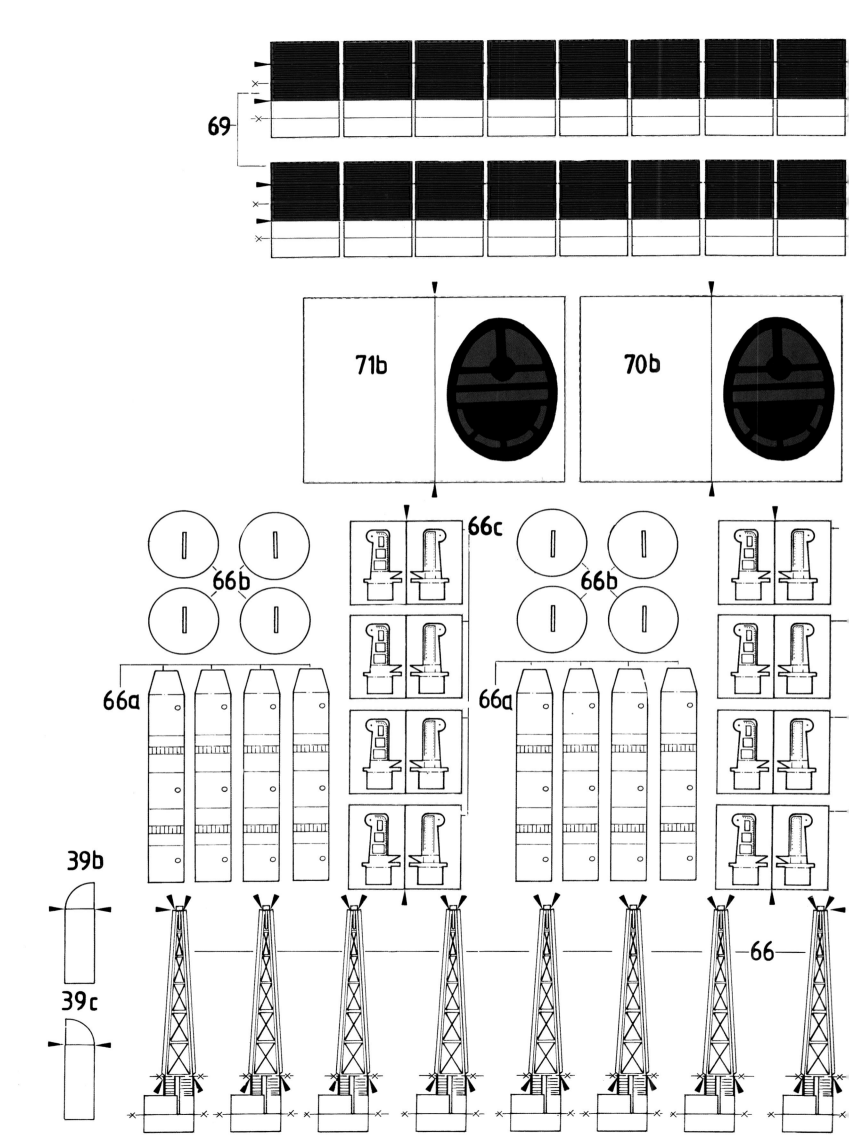

69

71b 70b

66c

66b 66b

66a 66a

39b

39c

66

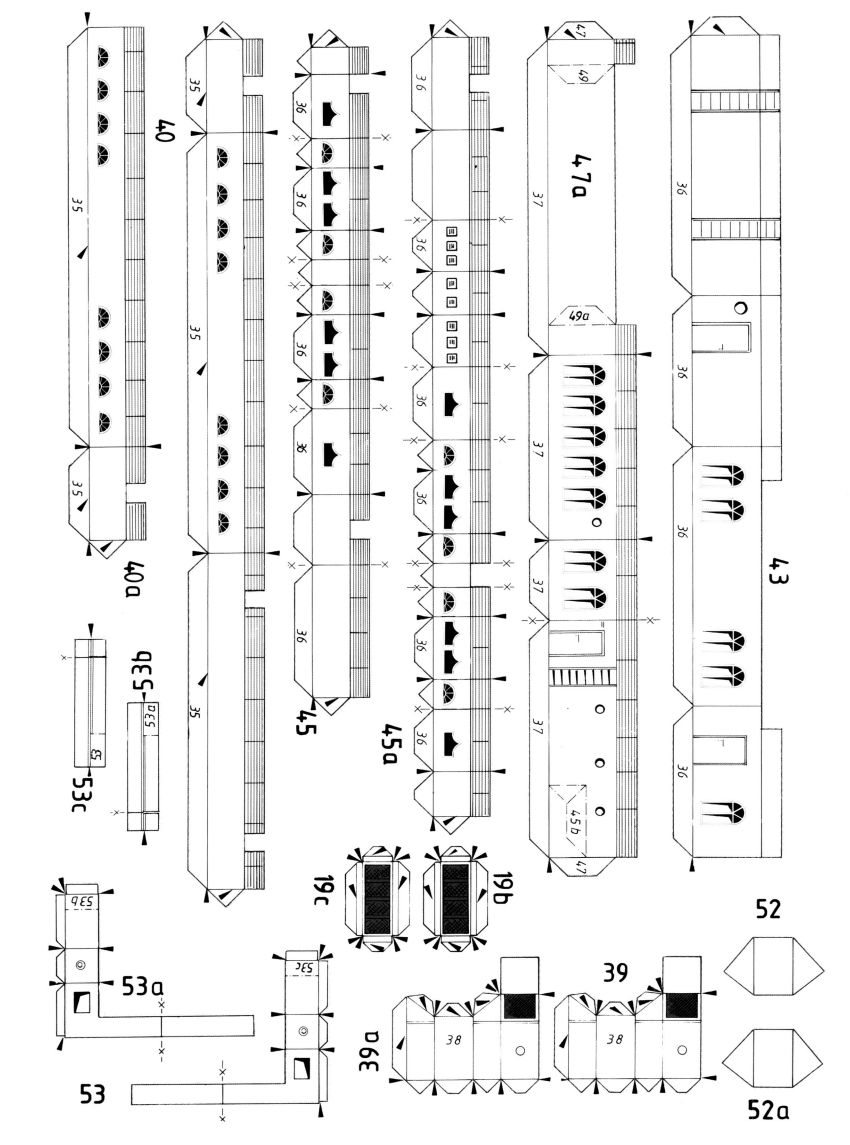

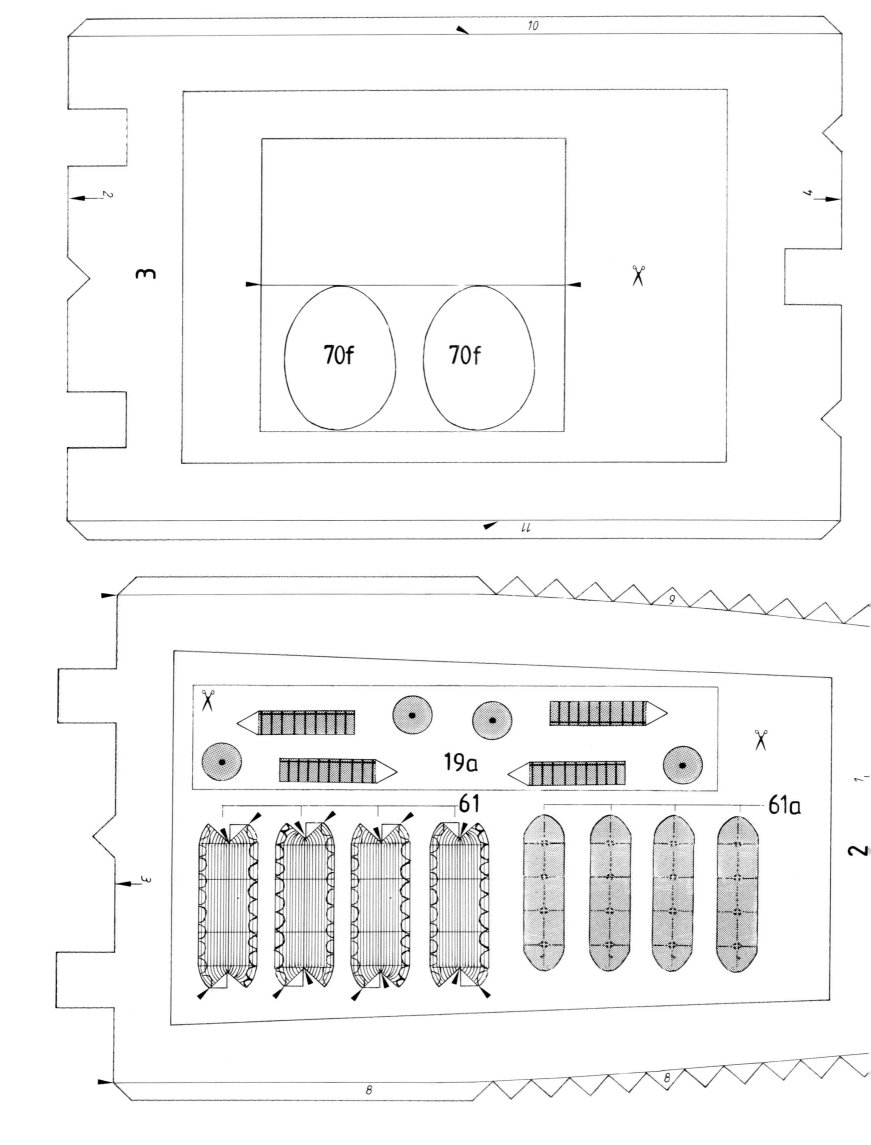

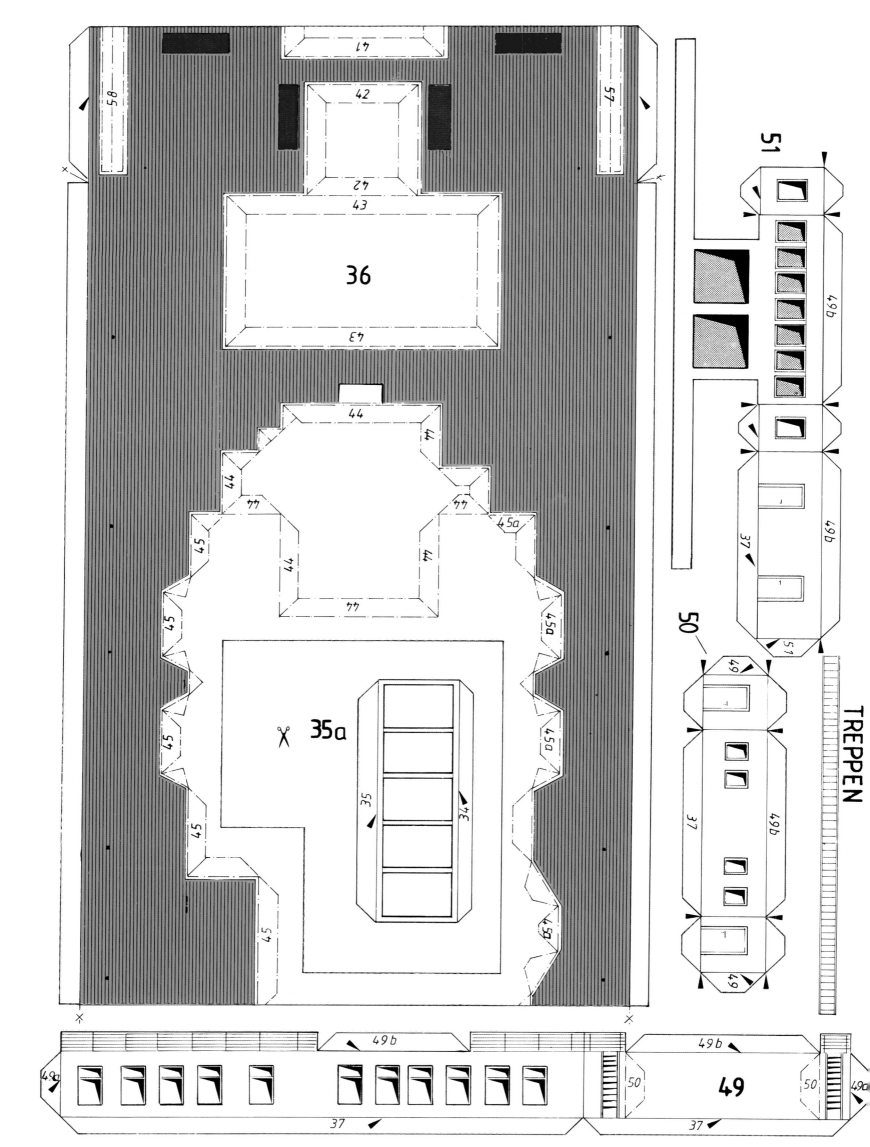

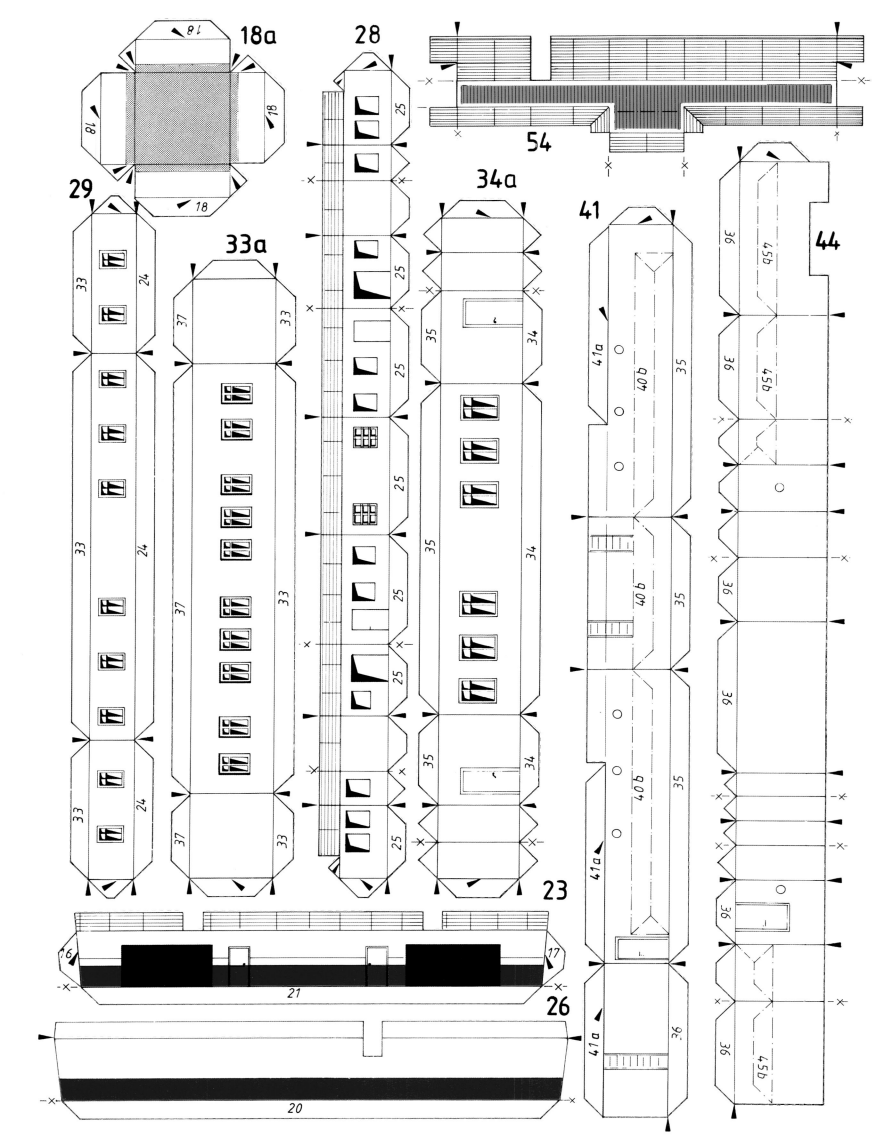

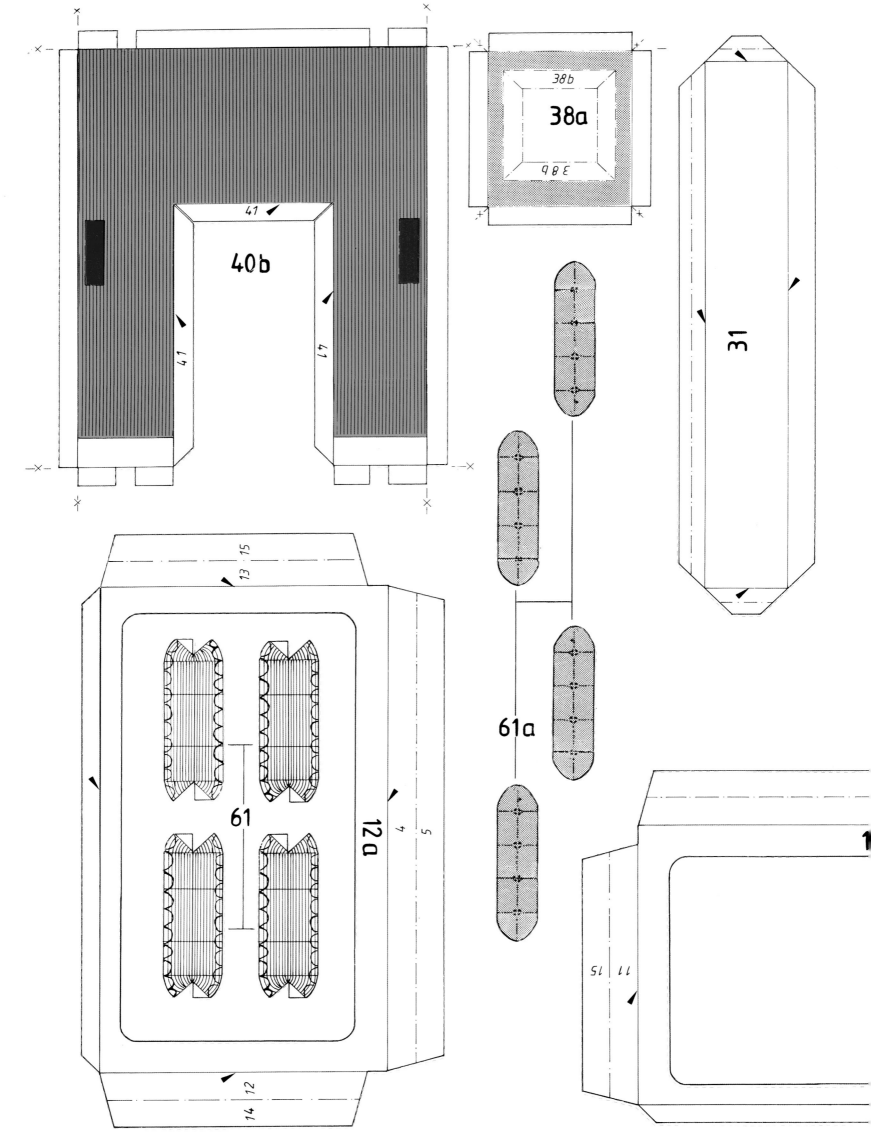

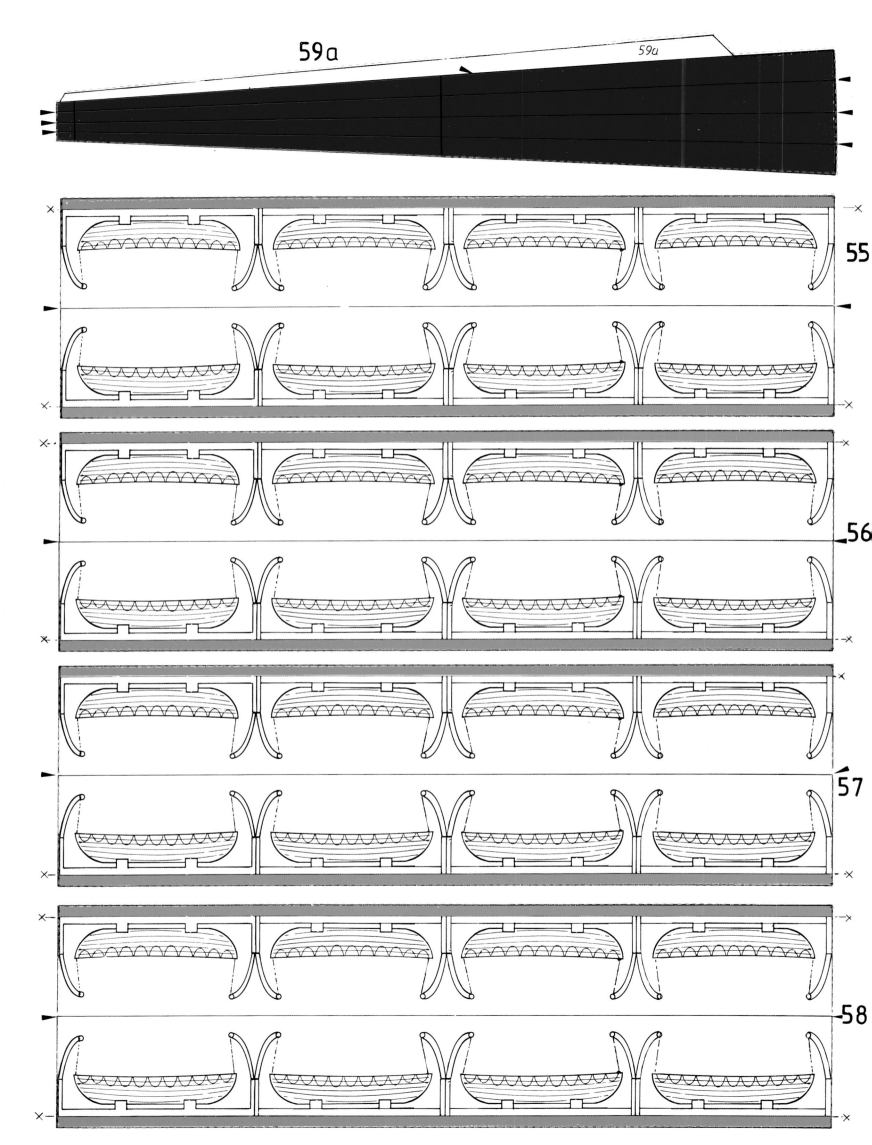

59a

59a

55

56

57

58

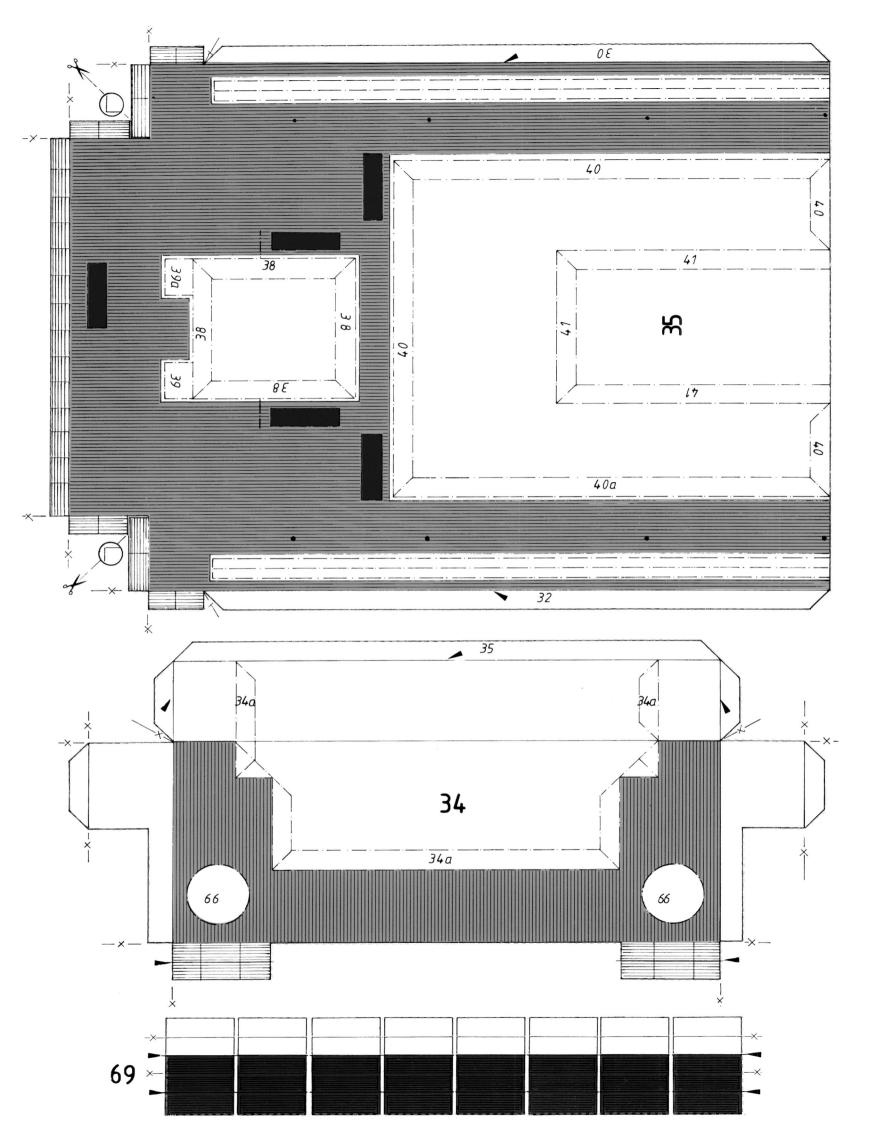

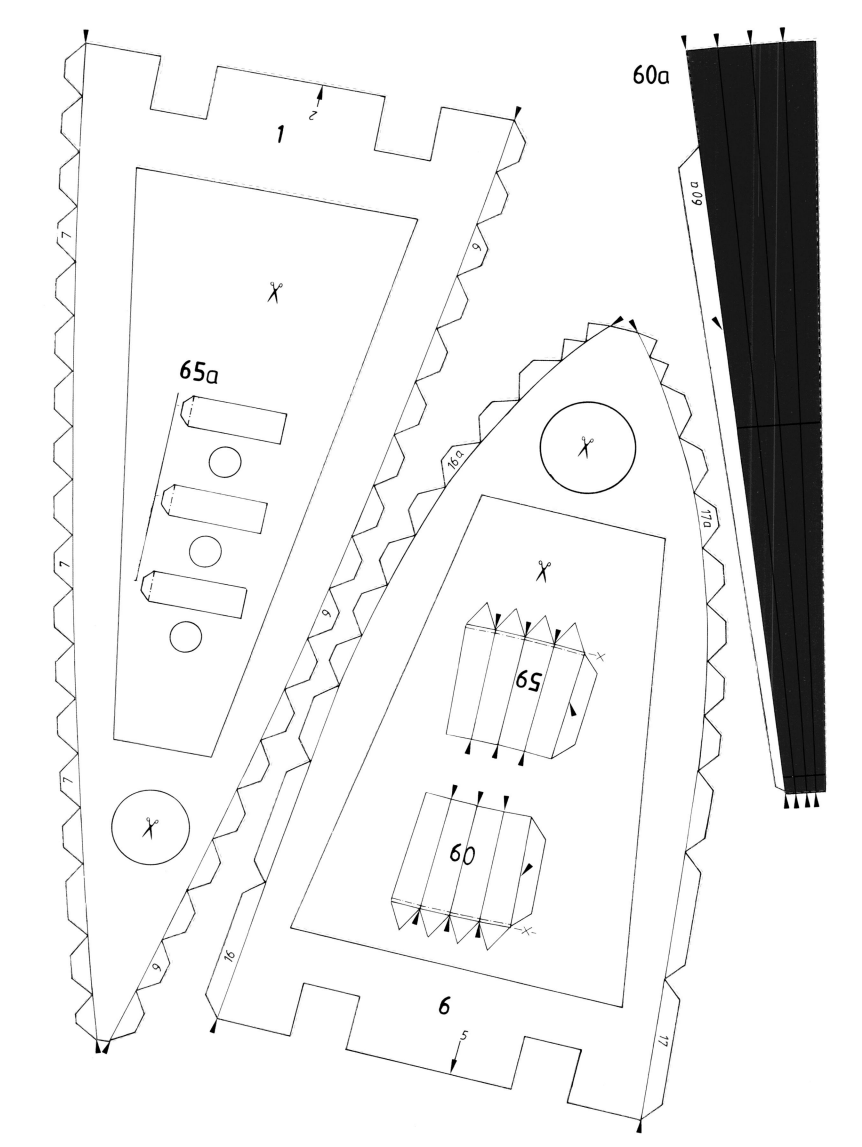

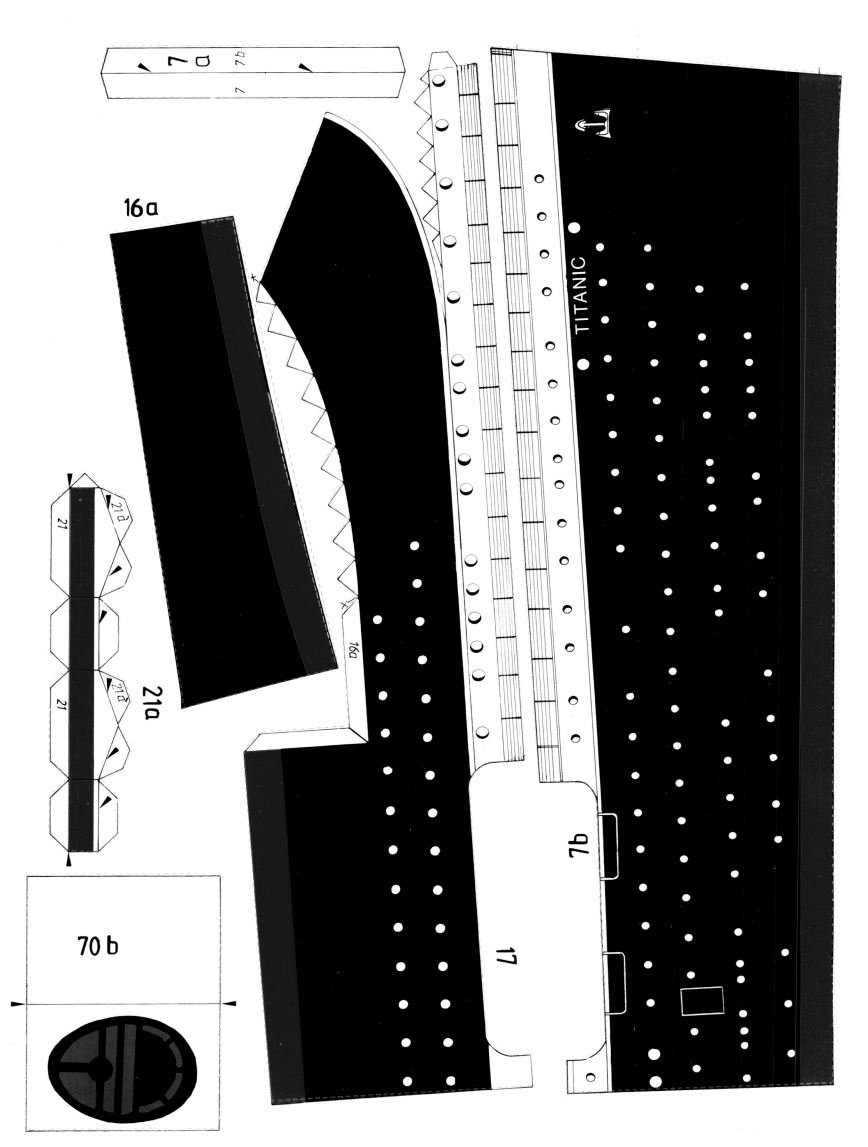

16a

21a

7

7b

70 b

TITANIC

7b

16a

21

21a

21

21a

17

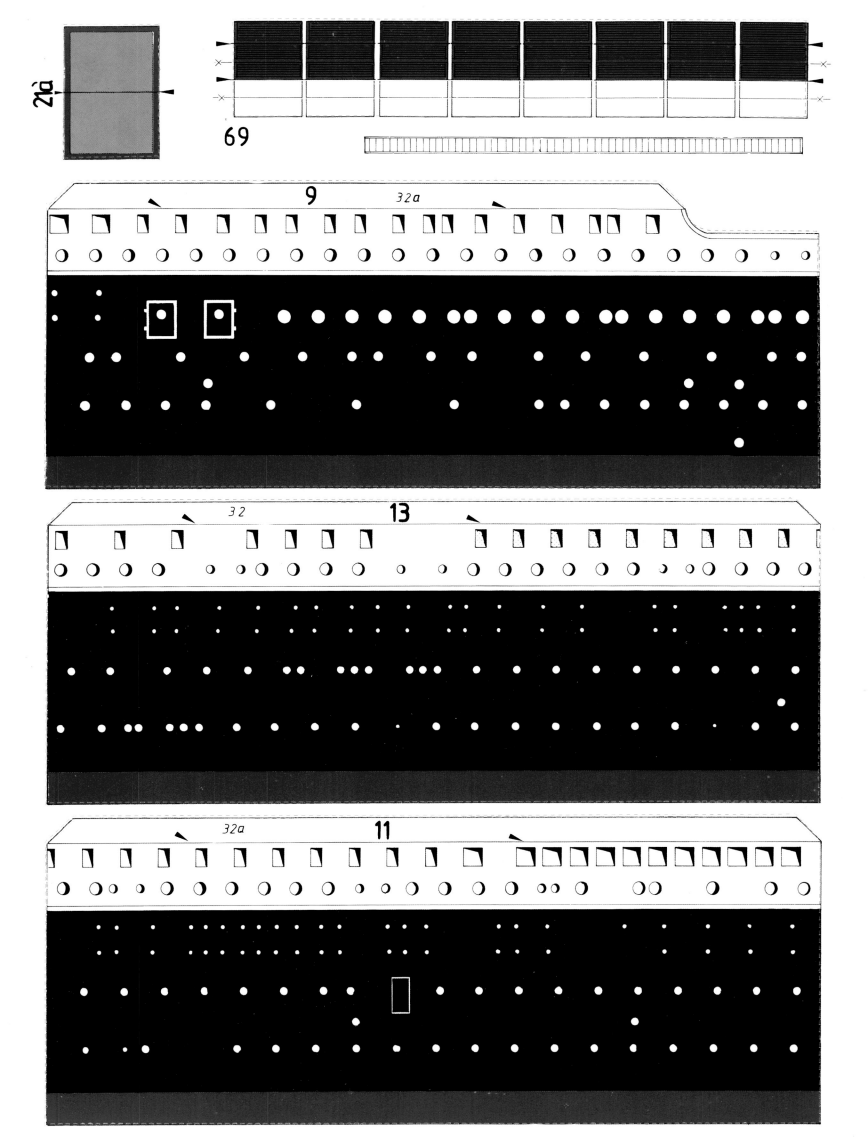

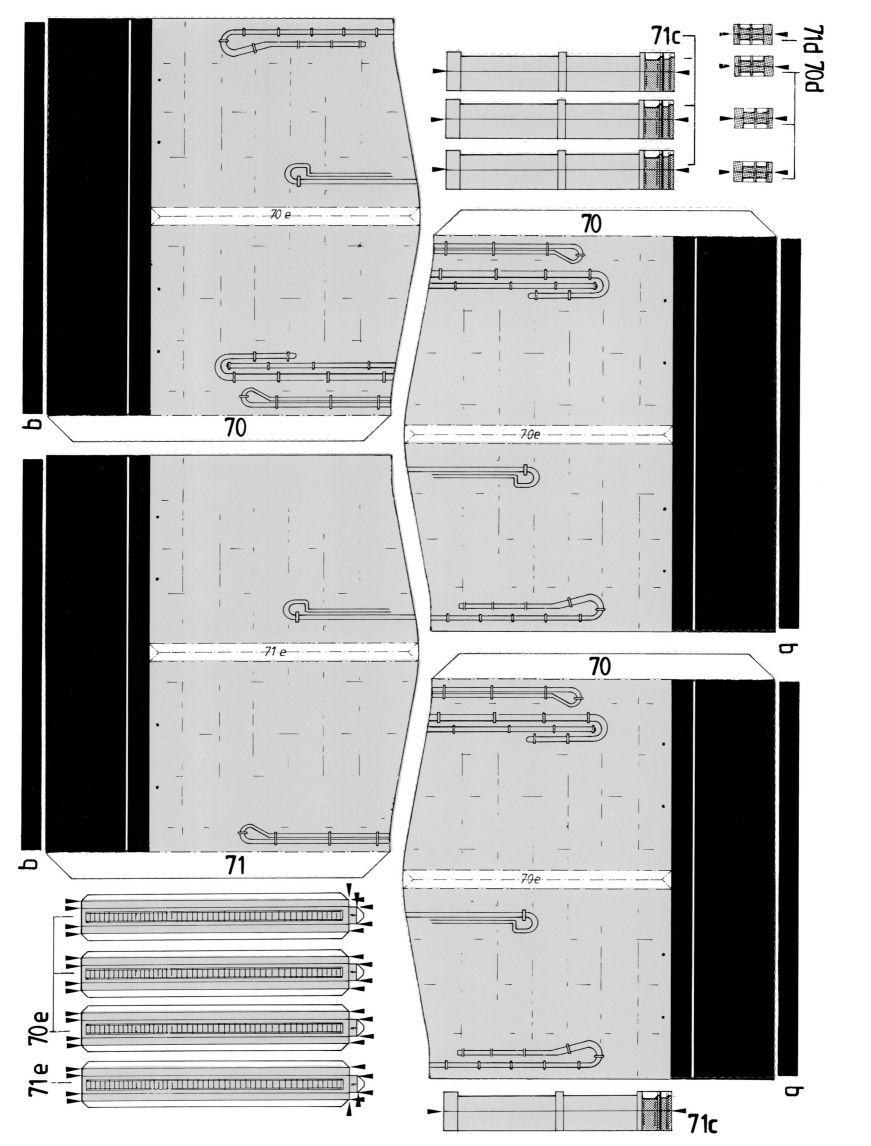

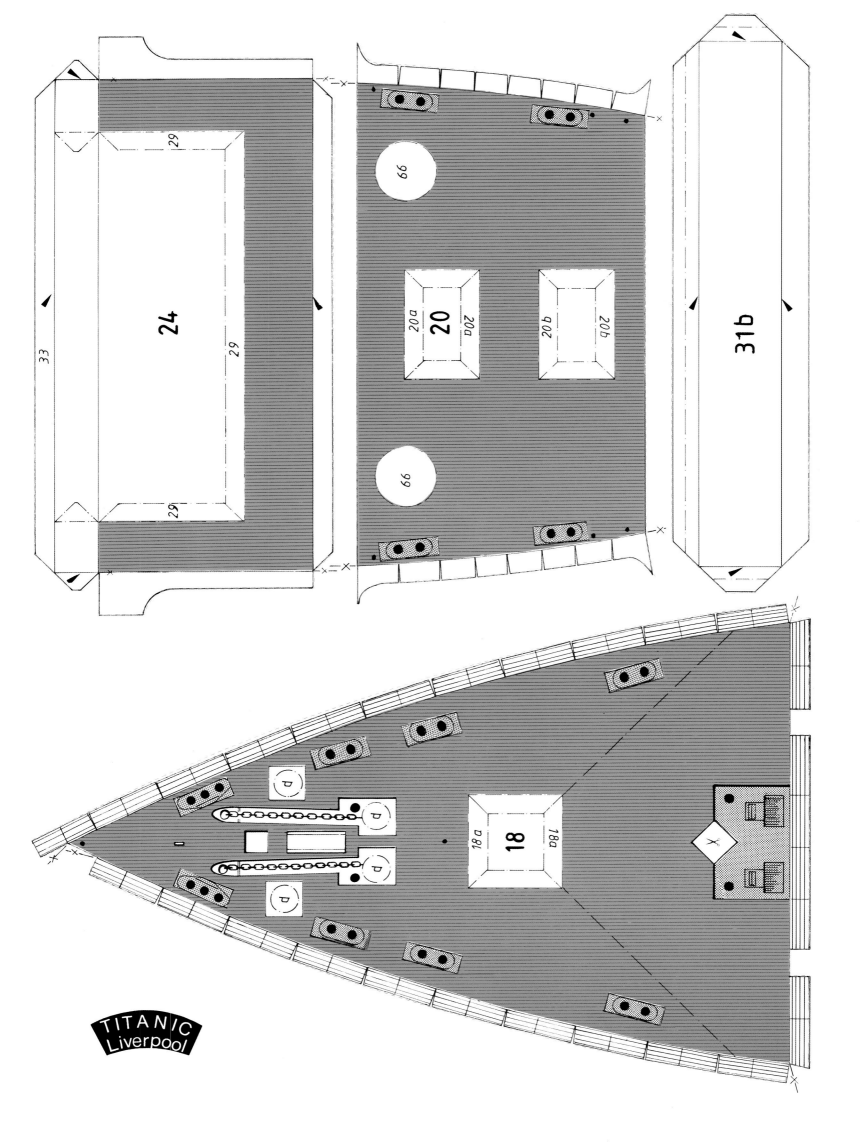

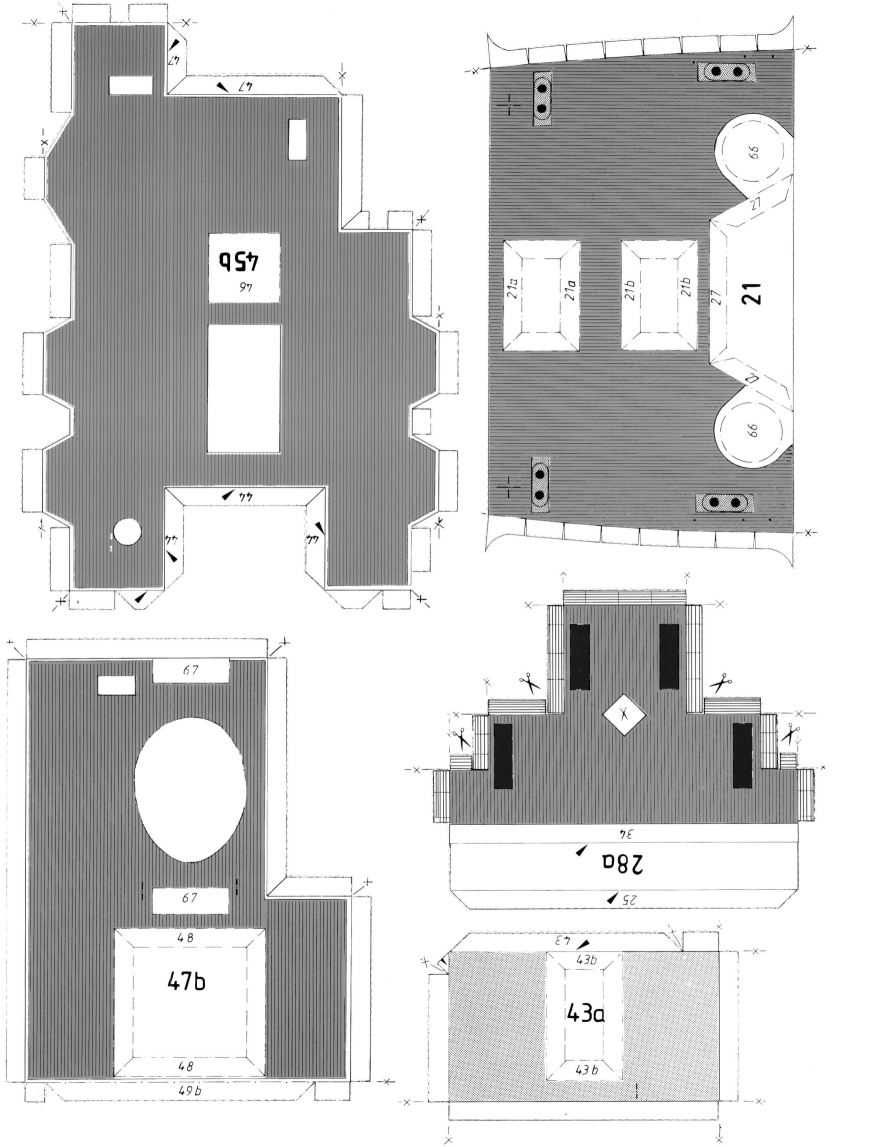

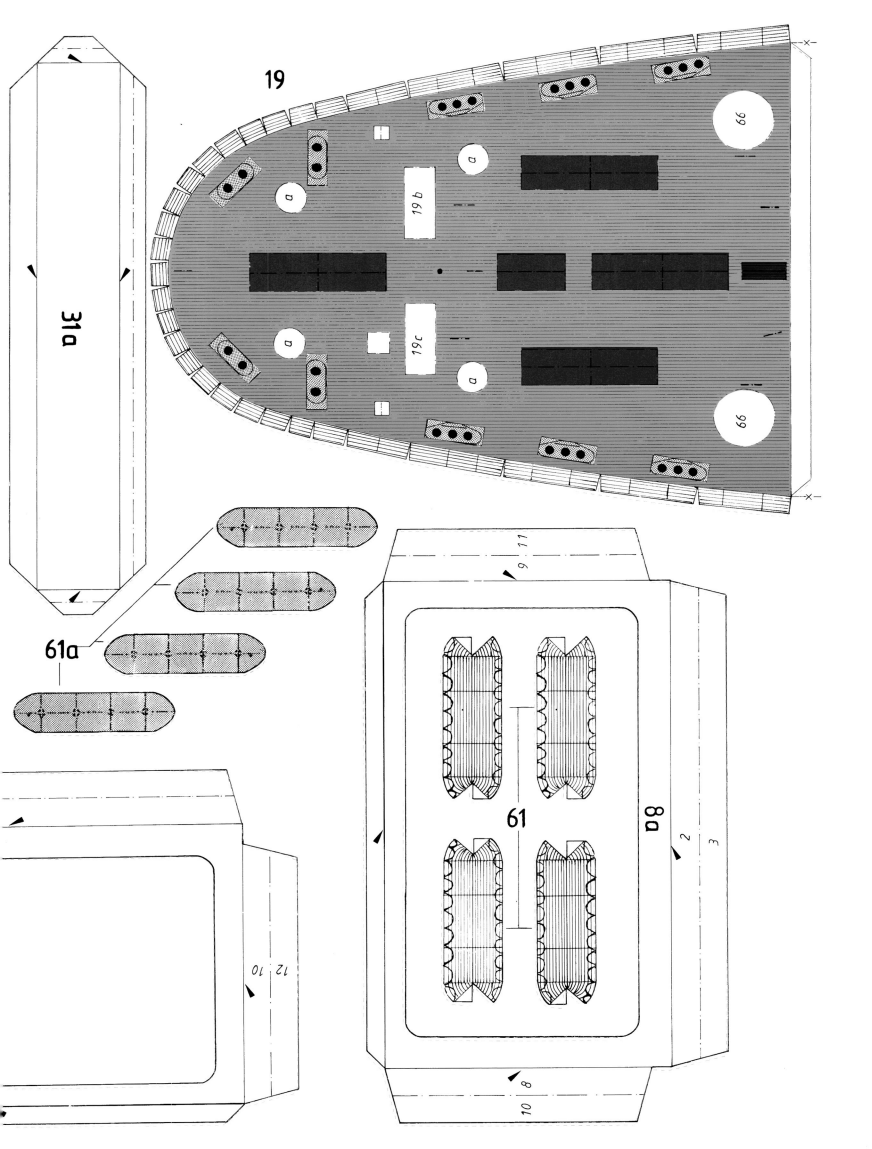

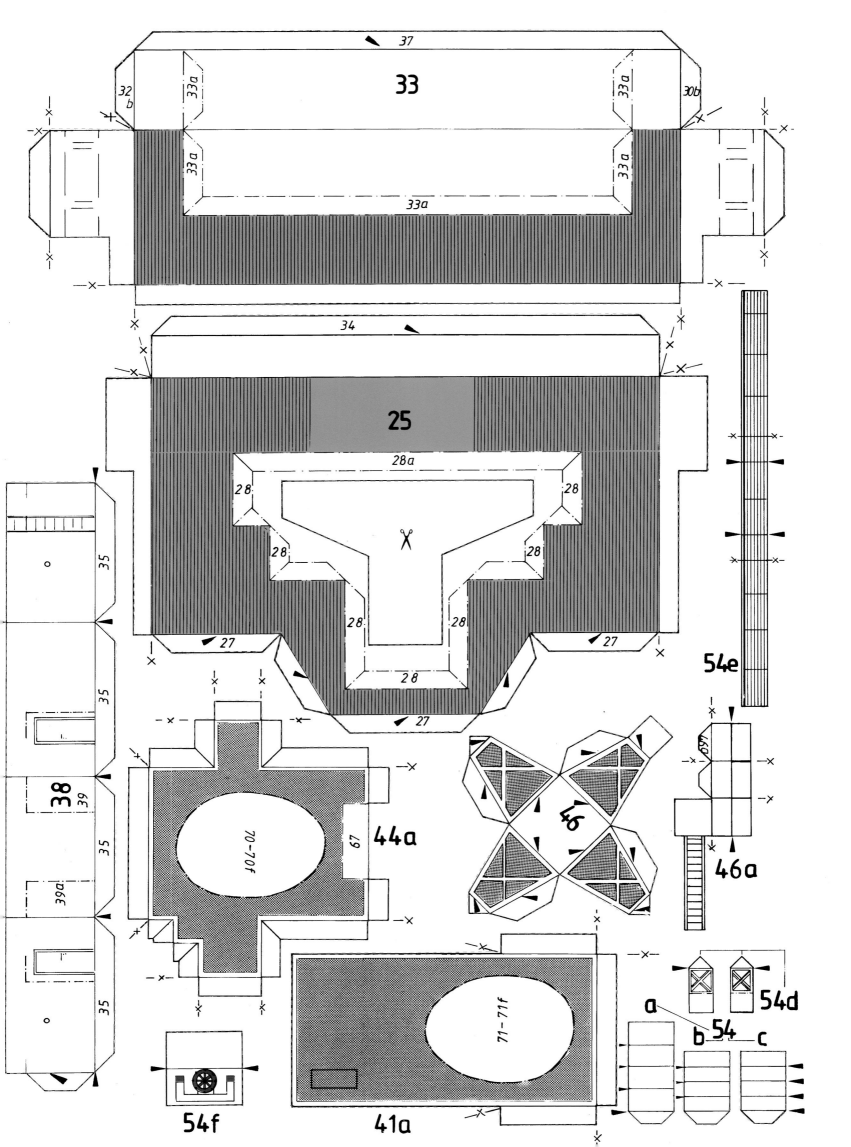

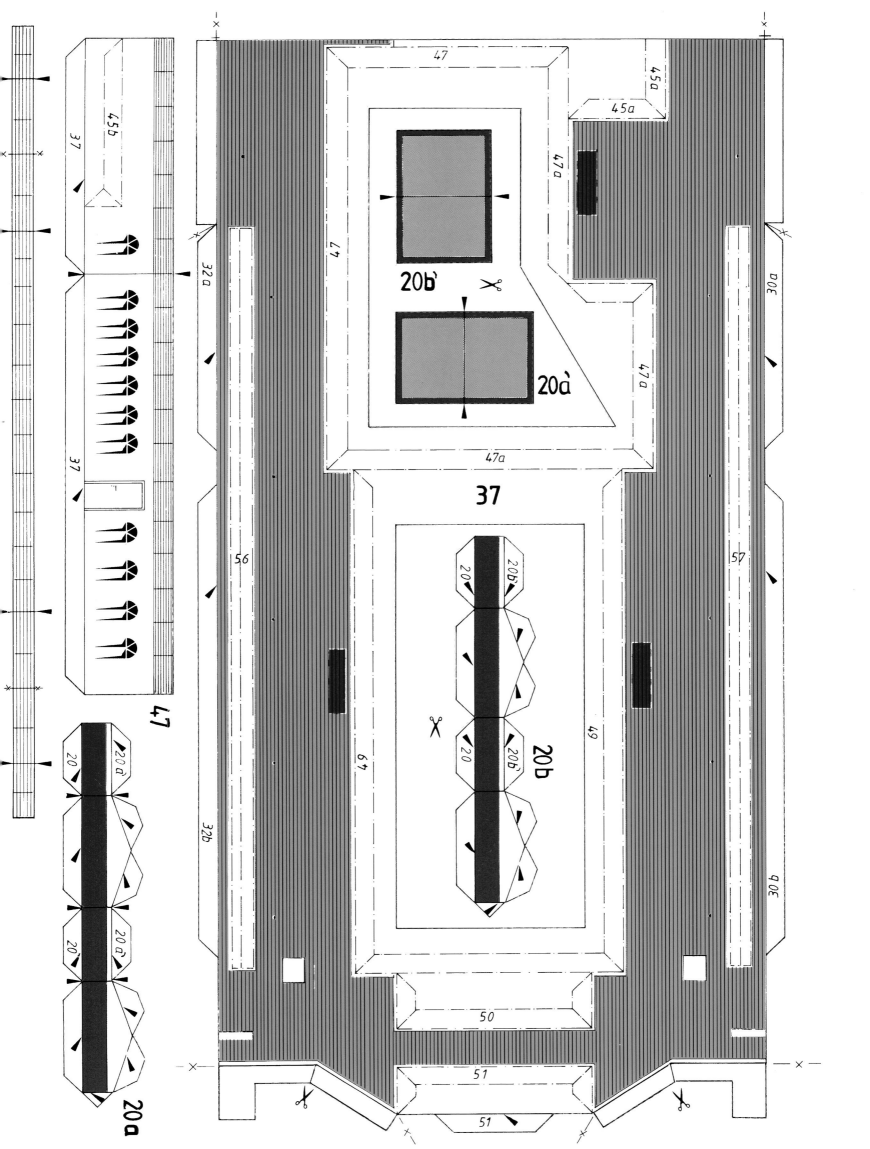

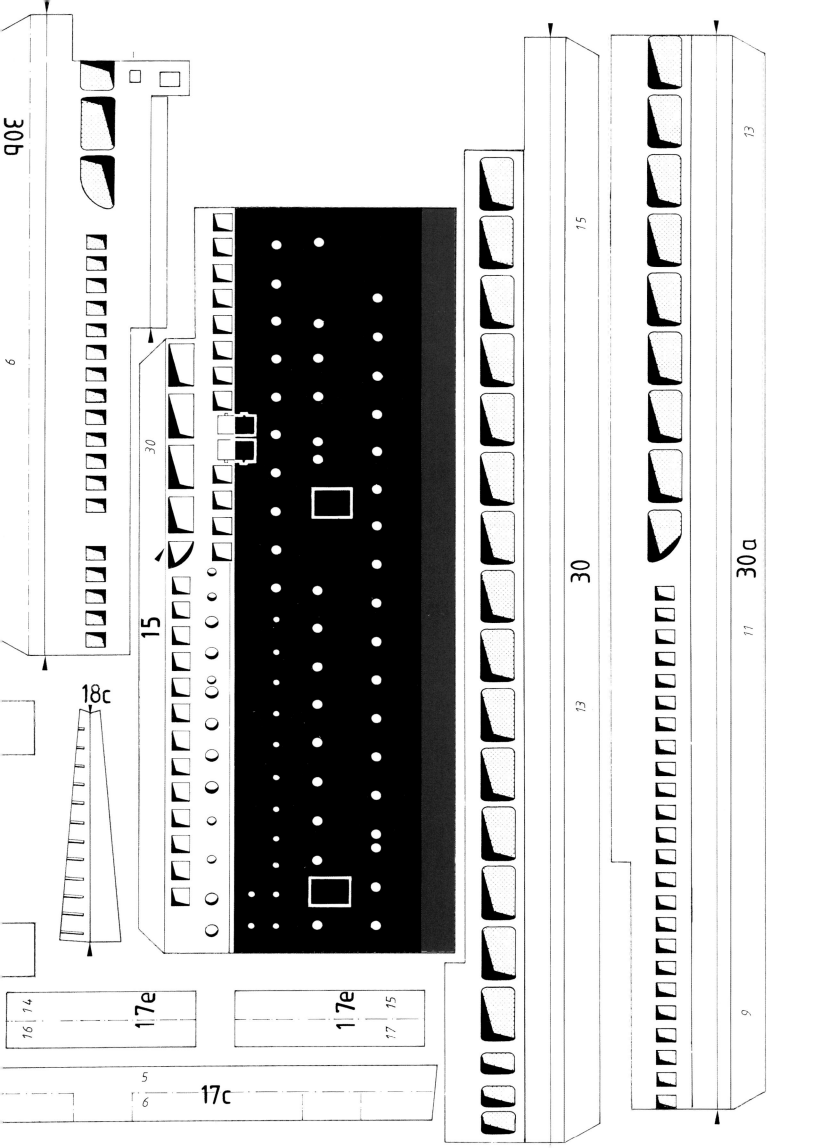

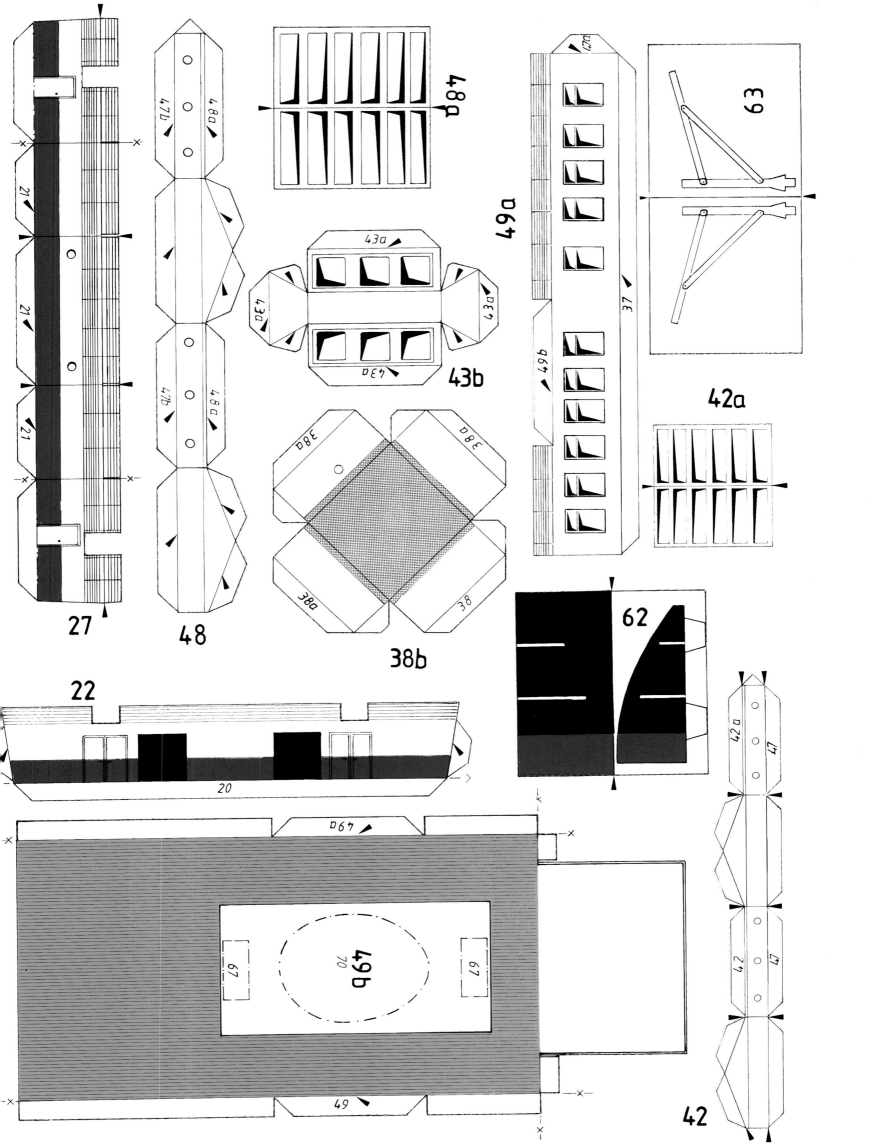

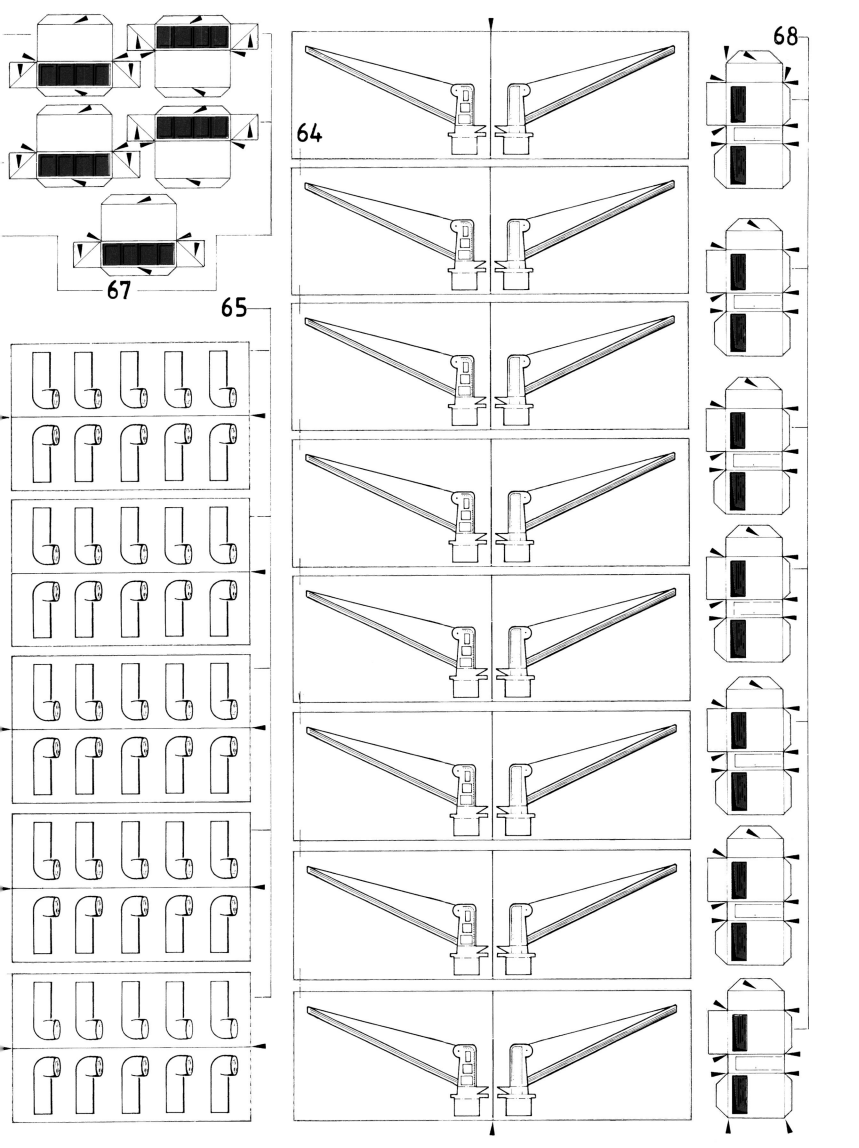

64

65

67

68

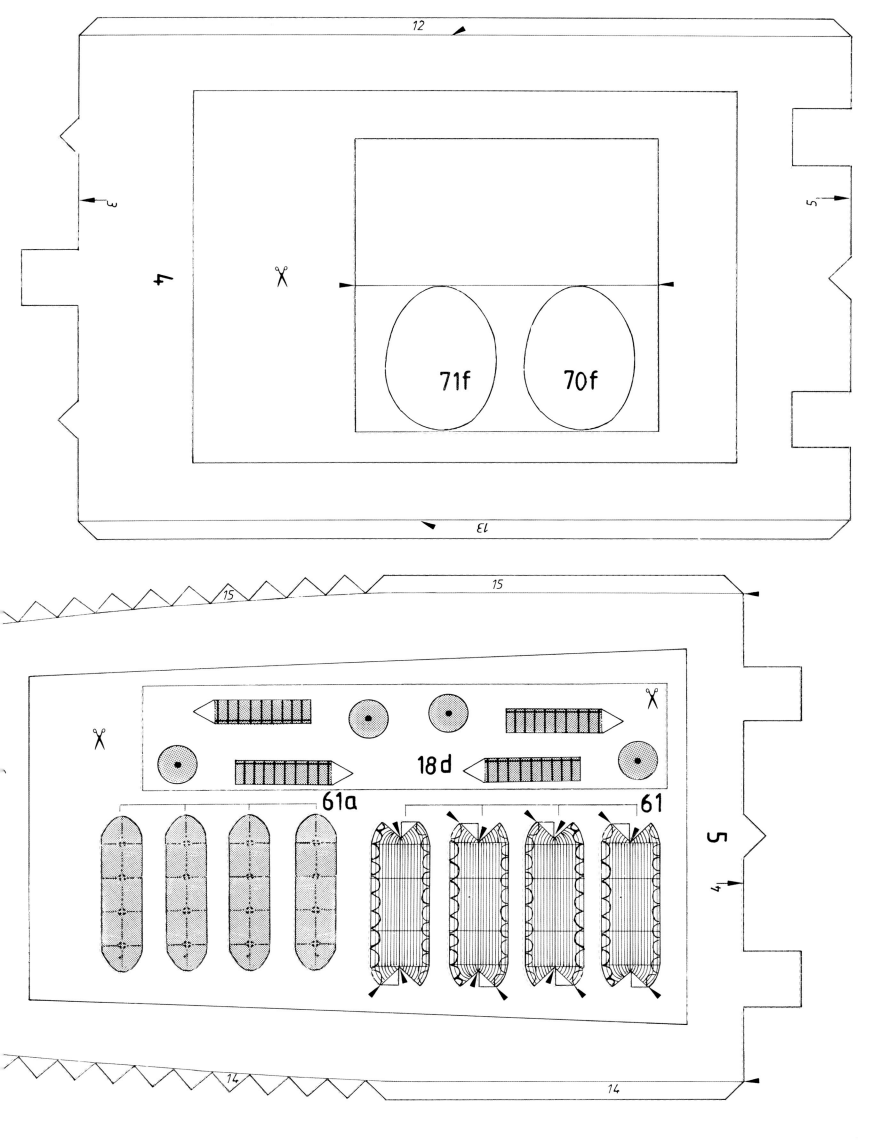

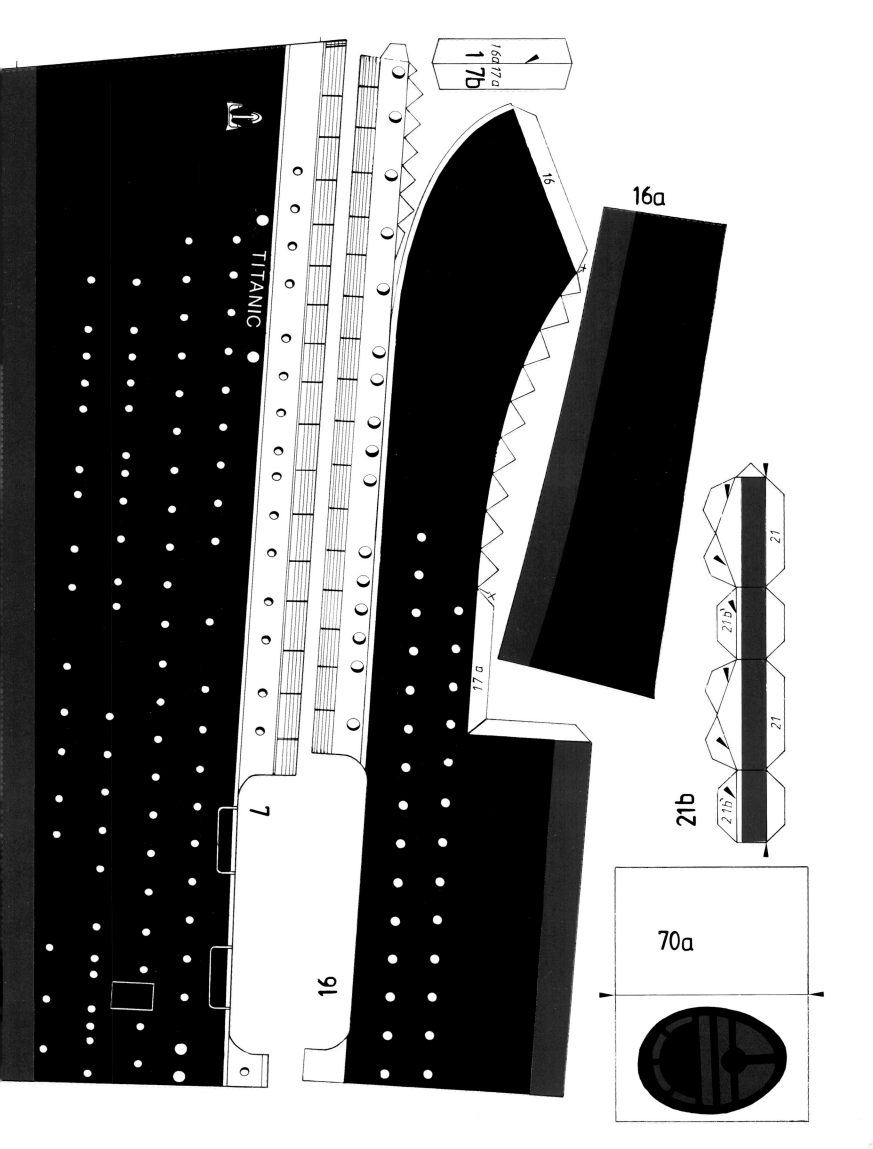

TITANIC

16a17a
17b

16

16a

17a

16

7

21b
21b'
21
21
21b'
21b

70a

bottles that could even be identified by their shapes: Madeira, Port, Champagne and Bordeaux. In 1986 Ballard launched another expedition into the depths of the sea: In a submarine he went down to the ship himself so that, with the help of a robot, he could have an even closer look. On eleven trips of four hours each he explored the wreck with a remarkable degree of thoroughness. Nearly two and a half miles under the surface of the Atlantic, at a pressure of almost 400 atmospheres, the searchlights flitted through the perpetual darkness. Using special, highly sensitive film, the expedition took some 6000 photographs and made 60 hours of video recordings. Controlled from the submarine, the robot could even penetrate into the ship itself and capture details of the interior on film.

However, the final fate of the *Titanic* has yet to be decided. The wreck and its treasures still have not been salvaged, and it will therefore continue to attract numerous adventurers and treasure-hunters.

1986 unternahm Ballard eine weitere Expedition in die Tiefe: Er tauchte selbst in einem Boot zum Wrack hinab, um es mit Hilfe eines Roboters noch genauer als bisher zu untersuchen. In elf Tiefseefahrten von je vier Stunden Dauer erkundete er das Wrack mit einer bemerkenswerten Gründlichkeit. Fast vier Kilometer unter der Oberfläche des Atlantiks, bei fast 400 Atmosphären Druck, geisterten die Scheinwerfer durch die ewige Nacht, und mit Spezialfilmen von höchster Lichtempfindlichkeit nahm die Expedition 6000 Fotos und 60 Stunden Video-Material auf. Der Roboter konnte sogar, vom U-Boot aus gesteuert, in das Innere des Wracks gelenkt werden, um dort Aufnahmen zu machen.

Allerdings ist das endgültige Schicksal der *Titanic* noch immer nicht entschieden. Die Bergung des Wracks und seiner Schätze steht noch aus. Es bleibt also die Verlockung für zahlreiche Abenteurer und Schatzsucher.

vait même identifier à leur forme : madère, porto, champagne ou bordeaux. En 1986, Ballard entreprit une autre expédition sous-marine : il descendit jusqu'à l'épave pour pouvoir l'observer de plus près à l'aide d'un robot. Au cours de onze plongées de quatre heures chacune, il explora l'épave avec une minutie remarquable. À environ quatre kilomètres au-dessous de la surface de l'Atlantique et sous une pression de 400 atmosphères, les projecteurs erraient à travers la nuit éternelle. Guidé depuis le sous-marin, le robot pouvait être dirigé à l'intérieur de l'épave. L'utilisation de pellicules très sensibles à la lumière permit à l'expédition de rapporter six mille photos et soixante heures de vidéo.

Nul ne sait aujourd'hui quel sera le destin de l'épave du *Titanic*. Du fond de l'océan, elle continue à attirer les aventuriers et les chasseurs de trésors...

Left: 711 survivors were rescued by the Cunard steamer Carpathia *under Captain Arthur Henry Rostron, which reached the scene of disaster at around 4 a.m. on 15 April: one of the* Titanic's *lifeboats rowed towards the* Carpathia.

Links: Bergung von 711 Überlebenden durch den Cunard-Dampfer Carpathia *unter Kapitän Arthur Henry Rostron, der am 15. April um 4 Uhr früh an der Unglücksstelle eintraf: Schiffbrüchige ruderten in Rettungsbooten zur* Carpathia.

À gauche : Sauvetage de 711 rescapés par le Carpathia, *paquebot de la Cunard Line commandé par le capitaine Arthur Henry Rostron qui arrive sur les lieux du naufrage le 15 avril à 4 heures du matin : des naufragés rament vers le* Carpathia *dans leurs canots de sauvetage.*

Right: Two hours after the catastrophe, the steamship Carpathia *took the first of the 711 survivors aboard: 338 men (20 % of all the men aboard), 316 women (74 % of the women) and 57 children (only 52 % of the children – most the children were in steerage, in poor families with a lot of children, where chances of survival were slimmest).*

Rechts: Zwei Stunden nach der Katastrophe nahm der Dampfer Carpathia *die ersten der 711 Überlebenden aus den Rettungsbooten auf – 338 Männer (20 %, aller Männer an Bord), 316 Frauen (74 % der Frauen) und 57 Kinder — also nur 52 Prozent der Kinder an Bord, vermutlich, weil die kinderreichen Familien vor allem in der dritten Klasse reisten, wo die Chancen auf Rettung schlechter waren.*

À droite : Deux heures après la catastrophe, le navire à vapeur Carpathia *prit à son bord les premiers des 711 rescapés ayant trouvé place dans les canots de sauvetage, soit 338 hommes (20 % des hommes à bord), 316 femmes (74 % des femmes) et 57 enfants (52 % seulement des enfants à bord, ceci tenant probablement au fait que les familles nombreuses voyageaient avant tout en troisième classe, où les chances de sauvetage étaient moindres).*

The disaster was reported worldwide in the illustrated press of the day. Here the front cover of La Domenica del Corriere, the Sunday supplement of the Italian daily newspaper Il Corriere della Sera of 28 April 1912.

Über die Katastrophe wurde in der damaligen illustrierten Presse weltweit berichtet. Hier das Titelbild der Sonntagsbeilage La Domenica del Corriere *der italienischen Tageszeitung* Il Corriere della Sera *vom 28. April 1912.*

La catastrophe fut amplement commentée dans la presse illustrée de l'époque. Illustration de couverture du supplément dominical La Domenica del Corriere *du quotidien italien* Il Corriere della Sera *du 28 avril 1912.*

Instructions

Materials and assembly tips

With these 12 sheets, you can build a scale model of what is probably the most famous ocean liner that ever sailed. While assembling the ship, you can feel like Thomas Andrews, the naval architect who designed the real *Titanic* (who, incidentally, also went down with her); but burdened by the knowledge that the majestic ship is now lying at the bottom of the ocean, 2 1/2 miles down. This haunted castle in Davy Jones' locker sank sometime between 11.39 p.m. on 14 April 1912 and 2.20 a.m. on 15 April.

For your "shipyard", you will need a few tools, whose use is described below.

Enjoy building your cardboard model!

Thomas Siwek / Designer

Knife

The most important tool. An X-Acto or similar knife, with replaceable blades, is particularly suitable. Such knives are available in all good graphics or model-building supply shops. A knife with snap-off blade segments is also suitable.

Scissors

Although all parts should be cut out with the knife mentioned above, scissors are also essential. You should have two on hand: a pair of medium-sized paper scissors, and a pair of small, straight scissors.

Ruler

This is essential when cutting or scoring edges.

Tweezers

For holding or pressing down very small or hard-to-reach parts.

Toothpicks

Wooden toothpicks or shashlik skewers are useful aids when applying and spreading glue in spots that are hard to reach. They are also excellent for removing excess glue that has oozed out of a joint.

Rod

Some pieces of this model must be curled. A wooden rod (diameter 4–5 mm, about ⅕ inch), or small knitting needles can be used for this purpose. Lay the piece face down in your palm or on your thigh, depending on its size, and roll the rod or stroke the needle across it. After curling, the piece can be shaped appropriately.

Adhesives

Transparent glue is needed, preferably in a dispenser that permits it to be applied one drop at a time. An extra-strength glue is also necessary for affixing the butted joints.

Paints

Watercolours (opaque) or felt-tip pens, while not necessary, will make the model's colouring brighter.

Cutting Surface

This should be smooth and clean. A special cutting pad sold for the purpose is a good investment; cuts in the surface close up again, so that it can be used for years.

For technical reasons only parts of the sheets have been punched.

Bauanleitung

Arbeitsmaterial und Hinweise

Aus den Ihnen hier vorliegenden zwölf Bastelbögen können Sie ein originalgetreues Modell des wohl berühmtesten Ozeanriesen der Welt anfertigen. Während Sie das Schiff zusammenbauen, fühlen Sie sich wie Thomas Andrews, der Konstrukteur der richtigen *Titanic* (er ist, nebenbei bemerkt, ebenfalls mit der *Titanic* untergegangen); allerdings sind Sie mit dem Wissen belastet, dass dieses herrliche Schiff in diesem Augenblick vier Kilometer tief unter der Meeresoberfläche versunken liegt. Ein Spukschloss auf dem Meeresgrund, das am 14. April 1912 zwischen 23.39 Uhr und dem 15. April um 2.20 Uhr versank.

Für Ihre „Schiffswerft" benötigen Sie noch einige Werkzeuge, deren Einsatz und Verwendung unten beschrieben werden. Ich wünsche Ihnen viel Spaß beim Zusammenbau!

Thomas Siwek / Konstrukteur

Schneidemesser

Das wichtigste Instrument; sehr geeignet sind ein NT-Cutter D 500 oder ein X-Acto-Messer. Beide Typen haben austauschbare Schneideklingen. Diese Cutter sind in allen guten Zeichenbedarfsgeschäften erhältlich. Für unsere Zwecke eignet sich aber auch jedes andere Schneidemesser mit Klingenstücken zum Ausbrechen.

Schere

Obwohl es sich empfiehlt, alle Teile mit dem oben erwähnten Schneidemesser auszuschneiden, sind Scheren für die Modellbauarbeit unersetzliche Werkzeuge. Man sollte zwei von ihnen bereitliegen haben: eine etwa mittelgroße Papierschere und eine kleine gerade Schere.

Lineal

Es wird unbedingt zum Anlegen an Schneide- und Ritzkanten benötigt.

Pinzette

Sie ist zum Halten bzw. Andrücken sehr kleiner oder unzugänglicher Bauteile erforderlich.

Zahnstocher

Holzzahnstocher und Holzschaschlikspießchen sind nützlich beim Auftragen und Verteilen von Klebstoff an unzugänglichen Stellen; auch zum Entfernen von herausgequollenem Klebstoff sind sie bestens geeignet.

Rundholz

An diesem Modell müssen einige Teile gerundet werden. Man verwendet dazu entweder ein Rundholz (Durchmesser ca. 4–5 mm) oder Stricknadeln kleineren Durchmessers. Zum Runden legt man das entsprechende Teil, je nach Größe, entweder in die Handfläche oder auf den Oberschenkel und rollt bzw. fährt mit der Stricknadel über die Rückseite des Teils. Nach dem Runden kann das Bauteil entsprechend geformt werden.

Klebstoff

Aus Erfahrung empfiehlt sich ein Flüssigklebstoff. Bewährt haben sich Klebstoffe mit Verstreichkappen zum punktgenauen Dosieren. Weiterhin wird ein Spezialkleber für harte Flächen benötigt. Damit werden alle stumpf anzuklebenden Teile angebracht.

Farben

Wasserfarben (Deckfarben) oder Filzstifte werden eigentlich nicht benötigt, können aber verwendet werden, um das Modell noch prächtiger zu gestalten.

Schneideunterlage

Sie sollte eben und sauber sein. Wer etwas investieren möchte, sollte sich eine jener Unterlagen zulegen, bei der sich alle Einschnitte sofort wieder schließen. Solche Unterlagen halten jahrelang.

Aus technischen Gründen können die Bastelbögen nur teilweise ausgestanzt werden.

Instructions de montage

Matériel et conseils

À partir de ces douze planches, vous pourrez bâtir une maquette fidèle au célèbre géant des mers, et imaginer être, le temps du montage, Thomas Andrews lorsqu'il conçut le *Titanic* (lequel disparut avec lui lors du naufrage). Seulement, vous savez, vous, que ce magnifique bâtiment repose aujourd'hui, tel un château hanté sous-marin, à quelque 4 000 mètres de fond, après avoir coulé majestueusement dans la nuit du 14 au 15 avril 1912, entre 23 h 39 et 2 h 20.

Côté matériel, seuls quelques outils, dont l'utilisation est décrite ci-dessous, vous seront nécessaires.

Nous vous souhaitons de passer d'excellents moments avec cette maquette !

Thomas Siwek / Concepteur

Cutter

L'outil le plus important. Le cutter NT D-500 ou le couteau X-Acto, qui disposent de lames interchangeables, sont particulièrement appropriés. On peut se les procurer dans tous les bons magasins de modélisme. Tout autre cutter dont les lames peuvent être remplacées convient également.

Ciseaux

Bien qu'il soit conseillé de découper tous les éléments avec le couteau décrit ci-dessus, les ciseaux demeurent indispensables. Il en faudra deux paires : des ciseaux à papier de taille moyenne et de petits ciseaux droits.

Règle

Absolument nécessaire pour les lignes de coupe et d'incision.

Pince à épiler

Sert à tenir les éléments très petits ou difficiles d'accès, ou à exercer une pression sur ceux-ci.

Cure-dents

Des cure-dents ou des pics en bois seront utiles pour poser et étaler la colle aux endroits difficiles d'accès. Ils permettent aussi d'ôter la colle débordant des jointures.

Baguette de bois

Quelques éléments de cette maquette doivent être arrondis. À cette fin, on utilisera une baguette de bois arrondie d'un diamètre 4 à 5 mm, ou des aiguilles à tricoter de grosseur moindre. Pour arrondir un élément, on le pose, selon sa taille, dans le creux de la main ou sur la cuisse, puis on passe sur le dos de celui-ci la baguette ou l'aiguille à tricoter. On peut ensuite lui donner la forme désirée.

Colle

L'expérience fait recommander une colle munie d'un bouchon doseur. Une colle extra-forte est également nécessaire pour coller tous les éléments bord à bord.

Couleurs

La peinture à l'eau (couleurs opaques) ou les crayons feutres ne sont pas obligatoires. Toutefois, leur utilisation ajoutera à la beauté de la maquette.

Sous-main

Il devrait être plat et propre. À celui qui voudrait investir un peu, nous conseillons l'achat d'un sous-main en matière plastique souple, où les coupures se referment aussitôt. On peut ainsi l'utiliser plusieurs années.

Pour des raisons techniques, les feuilles cartonnées n'ont été qu'en partie prédécoupées.

Procedure

Numbering

THE PART NUMBERS (the numbers in Roman type) are printed on the corresponding parts where possible. Where this was not possible, these numbers are printed next to the corresponding parts. In the latter case, these numbers should be noted on the reverse of the piece.

THE REFERENCE NUMBER (the number in smaller italic type) indicates the position where the corresponding number in Roman type should go.

The sequence of the numbers corresponds generally to the order in which the parts should be assembled. Where there are several identical parts, the same number has been used for all.

Gluing

All parts that are to be glued to another part must be aligned carefully on the respective dot-and-dash line. The individual parts are designed to fit exactly. Some parts do not have tabs for gluing. These are glued edge-to-surface.

Symbols and Notes on Procedure

These are lines to be scored on the front, along a ruler. The arrows show which line should be scored. For the tags, the arrow points to the line; for scoring lines within the part, arrows at each end point to the line.

These are also lines to be scored, but on the reverse. Prick through the ends of such lines with the knife or a needle, then turn the part over and score it between the marks.

Such dot-and-dash lines are neither scored nor cut. They indicate the exact position where the part with the corresponding part number should go.

These marker arrows show how two parts should be joined.

All outlines are drawn with bolder lines, as are the contours of internal areas that must be cut out. The latter case is indicated by little scissor symbols, showing that something is to be cut out here.

Arbeitshinweise

Bezifferung

DIE BAUTEILNUMMERN (das sind die gerade stehenden Zahlen) wurden nach Möglichkeit auf die entsprechenden Bauteile gedruckt. Wo dies nicht möglich war, stehen diese Zahlen direkt neben dem zugehörigen Bauteil. In diesem Fall sollten Sie die Bauteilnummer auf der Rückseite des Bauteils notieren.

DIE REFERENZNUMMER (das ist die kleinere, schräg gedruckte Zahl) gibt an, welches Bauteil mit der entsprechenden geraden Zahl an die bezeichnete Stelle gehört.

Grundsätzlich entspricht die Reihenfolge der Zahlen der Reihenfolge des Zusammenbaus. Gibt es von einem Teil mehrere Exemplare, so tragen sie alle die gleiche Nummer.

Kleben

Es werden alle Teile, die auf ein anderes Teil geklebt werden, genau mit der dafür vorgesehenen strichpunktierten Linie in Deckung gebracht. Die einzelnen Bauteile sind passgenau konstruiert. Manche Bauteile haben keine Klebelaschen; diese werden stumpf, d.h. mit der Kante auf die Fläche geklebt. Hierfür eignet sich am besten ein Spezialkleber für harte Flächen.

Zeichen und Arbeitshinweise

Dies sind Ritzlinien, die auf der Vorderseite entlang eines Lineals angeritzt werden. Die Pfeile geben an, welche Linie geritzt werden muss. Bei Klebelaschen zeigt der Pfeil auf die Linie; bei Ritzlinien innerhalb des Bauteils liegen sich die Pfeile gegenüber.

Dies sind ebenfalls Ritzlinien, werden aber von der Rückseite her geritzt. Man durchsticht die Endpunkte solcher Linien mit dem Schneidemesser oder einer Nadel, wendet das Teil und ritzt zwischen den Markierungen.

Diese Linien, die strichpunktiert gezeichnet sind, werden weder geritzt noch geschnitten. Sie bezeichnen die Stelle, an die das Bauteil mit der entsprechenden Nummer gehört.

Diese Markierungspfeile geben an, wie zwei Bauteile aneinander gehören.

Alle Außenkonturen sind stärker gezeichnet. Dies gilt auch für Innenfelder, die herausgetrennt werden müssen. In diesem Fall sind kleine Scherensymbole angebracht, die anzeigen, dass hier ausgeschnitten wird.

Conseils pratiques

Numérotation

LES NUMÉROS DES ÉLÉMENTS DE MONTAGE (en caractères droits) ont été reproduits dans la mesure du possible sur les éléments correspondants. En cas d'impossibilité, on les a placés juste après l'élément correspondant. Dans ce cas, il est conseillé de noter le numéro au dos de l'élément auquel il se rapporte.

Le NUMÉRO DE RELATION (imprimé plus petit en italique) indique quel élément portant le même numéro imprimé en caractères droits convient à cet endroit.

En principe, l'ordre des numéros correspond à la chronologie du montage. Les éléments identiques portent le même numéro.

Coller

Positionner avec précision sur la ligne en pointillés prévue à cet effet les éléments devant être collés ensemble. Les éléments ont été conçus pour coincider parfaitement. Certains ne disposent pas de languettes de collage : on les collera en appliquant leur arête sur la surface de base. À cette fin, il est préférable d'utiliser une colle extra-forte, comme nous l'avons déjà indiqué.

Repères et conseils pratiques

Lignes d'incision sur le recto le long d'une règle. Les flèches indiquent quelle ligne doit être incisée. Pour les languettes de collage, la flèche indique la ligne. Pour les lignes à inciser sur un même élément, les flèches sont placées face à face.

Lignes d'incision, mais cette fois-ci au verso des éléments. Transpercer les extrémités de ces lignes à l'aide d'un cutter ou d'une aiguille, retourner l'élément et inciser entre ces marques.

Lignes en pointillés. Elle ne doivent être ni incisées, ni coupées. Elles indiquent l'endroit exact où doit être l'élément portant le numéro de montage correspondant.

Flèches de repère. Elles indiquent comment deux éléments doivent être ajustés l'un à l'autre.

Tous les contours extérieurs sont marqués d'un trait plus épais. Il en va de même pour les surfaces intérieures qui doivent être détachées. Pour ces dernières, on a utilisé de petits symboles représentant des ciseaux. Ils signalent l'endroit où il faut découper.

NOTE

At several points in building this model, simplified versions of various parts can be made. Since it was unfortunately not possible to present the two versions separately, they are described in the individual steps of assembly. So less experienced model-builders need not despair: it is not necessary to make every little deck crane and every bench. And the lovers of detail can really let themselves go – even putting in the rigging of the masts and the funnels.

Steps of Assembly

Step 1

Start by assembling Parts 1–6 to form the base. The indentations at the joints ensure that they will be connected in the right order. Besides, the marker arrows indicate how the parts of the base fit together.

NOTE: The interiors of the base parts must be cut out; the holes are needed so that you can reach into the model later.

When assembling the parts, stick the individual segments together with adhesive tape.

The base alone is enough to give you an idea of how huge your model of the *Titanic* will be. It is advisable to have a sufficiently long tabletop available, at least until the ship's hull is more or less stable. Until then, the work surface should be level.

ACHTUNG

Beim Zusammenbau dieses Modells können Sie an mehreren Stellen, vereinfachte Versionen einzelner Bauteile verwenden. Da es leider aus technischen Gründen nicht möglich war, diese beiden Versionen räumlich voneinander zu trennen, wird darauf innerhalb der einzelnen Schritte gesondert hingewiesen.

Weniger geübte Bastler brauchen also nicht zu verzweifeln – nicht jeder kleine Ladekran und jede Sitzbank muss angefertigt werden. Hingegen hat der Detailfan jegliche Möglichkeit, sich an diesem Modell auszutoben; bis hin zur Vertäuung der Kamine und Masten.

Arbeitsschritte

Schritt 1

Wir beginnen damit, den Grundriss aus den Teilen 1–6 zusammenzufügen. Durch die Ausbuchtungen an den Schnittstellen ist immer nur eine Richtung möglich. Außerdem geben die Markierungspfeile an, wie die Grundplattenteile aneinander gehören.

ACHTUNG: Die Grundplatteninnenteile müssen ausgeschnitten werden. Die verbleibenden Löcher sind nötig, um später in das Modell greifen zu können.

Beim Zusammenlegen der Teile werden die einzelnen Segmente mit einem Klebestreifen zusammengeklebt.

Schon bei den Arbeiten am Grundriss bekommen Sie eine Vorstellung davon, wie riesig Ihre *Titanic* einmal werden wird. Es ist empfehlenswert, eine ausreichend lange Tischplatte zumindest so lange zur Verfügung zu haben, bis der Rumpf des Schiffes einigermaßen stabil zusammengebaut ist. Bis es soweit ist, sollte die Unterlage eben sein.

ATTENTION

À plusieurs endroits, une version simplifiée de montage des éléments est possible. Des raisons techniques ne nous ont pas permis de présenter à part cette version simplifiée, mais les alternatives sont mentionnées aux différentes étapes de montage. Les modélistes débutants n'ont donc aucune raison de désespérer : il n'est pas indispensable de confectionner chaque petite grue de chargement et chaque banc. En revanche, avec cette maquette, le fanatique de détails pourra s'en donner à cœur joie... jusqu'à consolider avec des filins les cheminées et les mâts !

Étapes de la construction

Étape 1

Nous commençons par assembler la charpente à partir des éléments 1–6. Les avancées sur les lignes de coupe montrent qu'une seule direction est possible. De plus, les flèches de repère indiquent l'agencement des socles.

ATTENTION : Les parties intérieures des socles doivent être découpées. Les trous qui restent permettront plus tard d'accéder à l'intérieur de la maquette.

Pour assembler les éléments, collez les segments avec un trait de colle. La charpente vous donne déjà une idée des dimensions gigantesques de votre *Titanic*. Il est recommandé de disposer d'une surface de travail assez longue et parfaitement plane, au moins jusqu'à ce que la coque du navire soit à peu près stable.

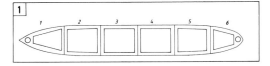
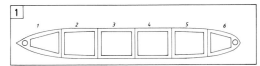
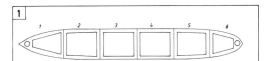

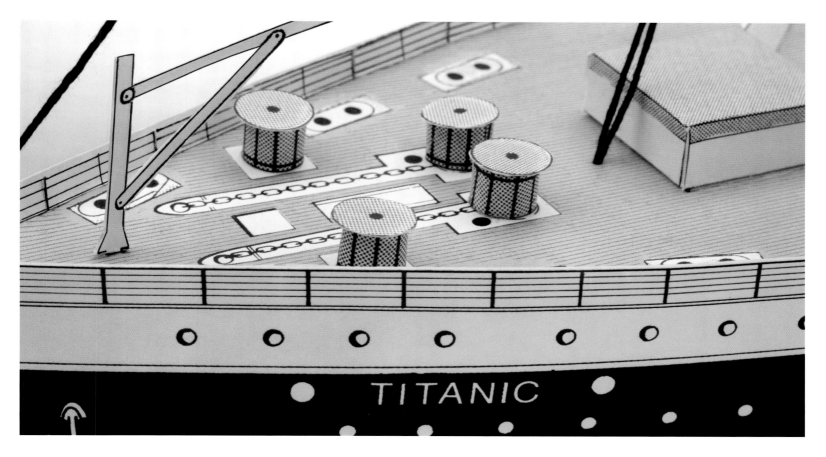

Step 2

Cut out parts 7–17, the ship's sides. If the part numbers are cut off, they should be marked on the reverse. It is especially important not to confuse the parts of the ship's sides, which are identical on port and starboard. Note the shadows cast in the portholes – these must always point in the same direction. Go by the numbers otherwise. Glue the side sections to the base one pair at a time; then insert the corresponding frame (Parts 8a, 10a, 12a). The frames serve to stabilize the hull. The parts fit precisely; be careful that nothing protrudes when you glue them together, and that the individual elements meet accurately. Curl the stern, (Parts 16, 16a, 17, and 17a).

Schritt 2

Für die Schiffswände Bauteile 7–17 ausschneiden. Wird die Bauteilnummer abgeschnitten, so sollte diese auf der Rückseite notiert werden. Gerade bei den beidseitig identischen Schiffswänden ist es sehr wichtig, die Seiten nicht zu vertauschen. Man beachte den Schattenwurf in den Fenstern – er muss immer in die gleiche Richtung weisen. Im Übrigen orientiere man sich an der Bezifferung. Die Seitenwände werden immer jeweils paarweise gegenüberliegend an den Grundriss geklebt, dann werden die zugehörigen Spanten (Bauteile 8a, 10a, 12a) eingefügt. Ein Spant dient zur Stabilisierung des Schiffsrumpfes. Die Bauteile passen genau aneinander; achten Sie beim Zusammenkleben darauf, dass keine Überhänge auftreten und dass die einzelnen Elemente genau aneinander liegen. Das Heck (Bauteile 16, 16a und 17, 17a) rund formen.

Étape 2

Découper les parois du navire (éléments 7–17). Si vous coupez le numéro de l'élément de montage, notez-le au dos de celui-ci. En effet, il est très important de ne pas confondre les côtés des parois qui ont deux faces identiques. Pour ce, veiller à ce que l'ombre qui tombe sur les fenêtres soit toujours dans la même direction. D'autre part, s'en remettre à la numérotation. Coller les parois transversales sur la charpente toujours en face l'une de l'autre. Introduire alors le couple correspondant (éléments 8a, 10a, 12a). Un couple sert à stabiliser la coque du navire. Les éléments étant très précisément conçus, veiller à ce qu'un élément ne déborde pas sur l'autre et à ce que les jointures coincident parfaitement. Arrondir la poupe (éléments 16, 16a, 17 et 17a).

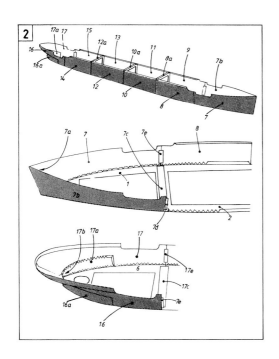
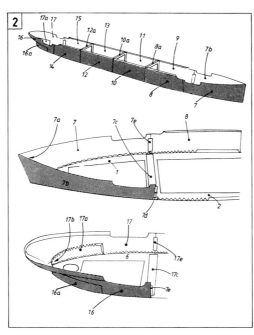
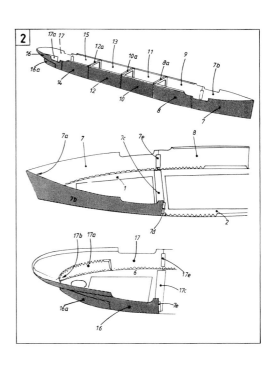

Step 3

Now the *Titanic*'s hull is assembled. Cut out the decks at bow (Part 18) and stern (Part 19), score on the reverse, and glue them in place. Parts 18a (cargo hatch), 18b/c (splash guards) and 18d (for windlasses) can be finished now – but do not glue them on yet. The same applies to the bits and winches (19a) and ventilator coamings (19b/c).

NOTE: Cut out the hole in deck 18 for the foot of the mast.

Schritt 3

Nun steht bereits der Rumpf der *Titanic*. Das Deck am Bug (Bauteil 18) sowie das Deck am Heck (Bauteil 19) ausschneiden, rückseitig ritzen und einkleben. Die Bauteile 18a (Ladeschacht), 18b/c (Wasserschutz) und 4 x 18d (Ankerwinden) können schon einmal fertiggestellt werden – sie sollten allerdings erst später aufgeklebt werden.

Dasselbe gilt für die Poller und Winden 19a und die Luftschächte 19b/19c.

ACHTUNG: Bei Deck Nr. 18 das Loch für den Mastfuß ausschneiden!

Étape 3

La coque du *Titanic* est déjà finie. Découper le pont de proue (élément 18) et celui de la poupe (élément 19), inciser le dos de l'élément et coller. On peut monter la fosse de chargement (élément 18a), le pare-lame (élément 18b/c) et les guindeaux (4 x 18d), mais on ne les collera que plus tard. De même pour les bittes d'amarrage et les treuils (19a) et pour les puits d'aération (19b/19c).

ATTENTION : Pont n° 18 – découper le trou pour le pied du mât.

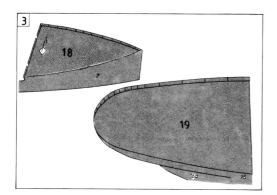
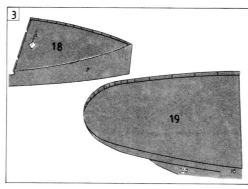
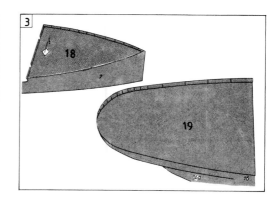

Step 4

Cut out the forward (Part 20) and aft (Part 21) well decks, score them on the reverse, and insert in the next section after the decks at bow and stern. Prepare the cargo hatches 20a/b and 21a/b; however, like the parts listed above, do not install them until the hull is complete.

Insert Parts 22 and 23 (outer walls) to connect the well decks and the decks at bow and stern – Part 22 forward, and Part 23 aft.

Step 5

We progress gradually from the two ends towards the middle of the ship. Cut out the 'tween decks, Parts 24 (forward) and 25 (aft), score them on the reverse, and insert. Parts 26 and 27 connect the 'tween decks just inserted with the well decks, No. 26 forward and No. 27 aft. Cut out and score the deck erections for the 'tween decks, Parts 28 and 28a aft and 29 forward, and glue them in place.

NOTE: Cut out the hole in deck 28a for the foot of the mast.

Schritt 4

Vorderes Welldeck (Bauteil 20) und hinteres Welldeck (Bauteil 21) ausschneiden, rückseitig ritzen und in der nächsten Stufe nach den Decks am Heck und am Bug einfügen. Die Ladeschächte (20a/20b sowie 21a/21b) werden vorbereitet, aber wie die schon oben aufgeführten Bauteile erst nach Fertigstellung des gesamten Rumpfes montiert.

Bauteile 22 und 23 (Wände) als Verbindung zwischen Welldecks und Vorder- bzw. Heckdecks einfügen. Bauteil 22 kommt an den Bug, Bauteil 23 ans Heck.

Schritt 5

Langsam arbeiten wir von den beiden Enden her zur Schiffsmitte vor. Die Zwischendecks Nr. 24 (vorn) und Nr. 25 (hinten) ausschneiden, rückseitig ritzen und einfügen. Die Bauteile 26 und 27 verbinden die soeben eingefügten Zwischendecks mit den Welldecks; Teil 26 vorn, Teil 27 hinten.

Die Deckaufbauten für die Zwischendecks (Bauteile 28 und 28a hinten sowie Bauteil 29 vorn) ausschneiden, ritzen, mit Klebstoff bestreichen und aufkleben.

ACHTUNG: Bei Deck Nr. 28a das Loch für den Mastfuß ausschneiden.

Étape 4

Découper le pont de lames avant (élément 20) et le pont de lames arrière (élément 21), inciser le dos des éléments et les introduire à l'étape suivante, après les ponts de poupe et de proue. Préparer les fosses de chargement (éléments 20a/20b et 21a/21b) mais ne les monter qu'une fois la coque terminée, comme pour les éléments précédents. Introduire les éléments 22 et 23 (parois) comme liaison entre les ponts de lames et les ponts avant et arrière. Poser l'élément 22 contre la proue, et l'élément 23 contre la poupe.

Étape 5

Des deux extrémités, nous passons peu à peu au milieu du navire. Découper les entreponts (entrepont avant : élément 24, entrepont arrière : élément 25), les inciser au dos et les insérer. Les éléments 26 et 27 relient les entreponts juste insérés aux ponts de lames, 26 à l'avant, 27 à l'arrière.

Découper, inciser et coller les superstructures pour les entreponts (éléments 28 et 28a à l'arrière, élément 29 à l'avant).

ATTENTION : Pont n° 28a – découper le trou pour le pied du mât.

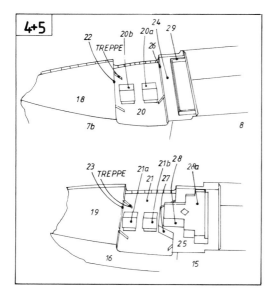
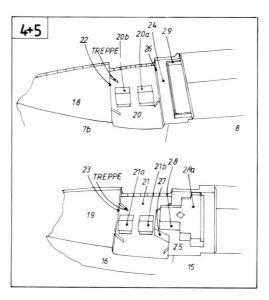
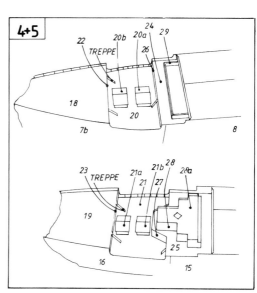

Step 6

Superstructure – outer upper promenade deck: glue Parts 30, 30a, and 30b onto the port side (right side viewed from the bow) of the *Titanic*, starting aft, and allowing the overlap provided. Make sure that the uppermost edge of the hull terminates aft with the rear edge of Part 30 (and of Part 32 on the other side). Assemble the promenade deck simultaneously on both sides, like the hull, with Parts 32, 32a, and 32b on the starboard (left seen from the bow) side.

There are three struts, 31, 31a, and 31b, two of which are used to connect the three superstructure components. The third can be installed later as desired when fitting the upper decks. The upper decks will then be supported by these three struts.

Schritt 6

Schiffsaufbau, oberer Wandelgang außen: Die Bauteile 30, 30a und 30b, vom Bug gesehen rechts, werden von hinten mit dem dafür vorgesehenen Überhang auf den Rumpf der *Titanic* geklebt. Dabei ist darauf zu achten, dass die obere Kante des Rumpfes hinten bündig mit der hinteren Kante von Teil 30 bzw. Teil 32 (auf der anderen Seite) abschließt. Auch der Aufbau des Wandelgangs wird, wie der Schiffsrumpf, auf beiden Seiten gleichzeitig vorgenommen. Es gibt insgesamt drei Verstrebungen: 31, 31a, 31b; zwei davon werden zur Verbindung der drei Aufbauelemente genutzt. Die dritte Verstrebung kann später, beim Einpassen der Oberdecks, nach Belieben angebracht werden. Auf diesen drei Verstrebungen liegen später die Oberdecks.

Étape 6

Superstructure du bateau : pont promenade supérieur extérieur. En commençant à l'arrière, coller les éléments 30, 30a, 30b – qui, vus de la proue, se situent à droite – à la coque du *Titanic* grâce au rebord prévu à cet effet. Veiller à ce que le bord supérieur de la coque joigne bien, à l'arrière, le bord arrière de l'élément 30, ainsi que de l'élément 32 situé de l'autre côté. Construire le pont promenade des deux côtés en même temps, comme la coque. Au total, il y a trois entretoises (éléments 31, 31a, 31b) ; deux d'entre elles servent à relier les trois éléments de la superstructure. On est libre d'insérer la troisième entretoise plus tard, lors de l'emboîtement des ponts supérieurs.

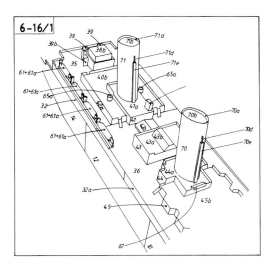

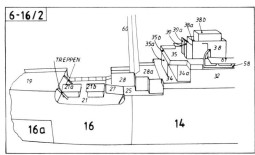

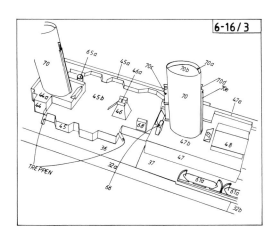

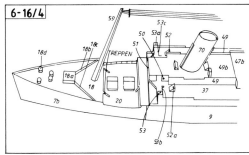

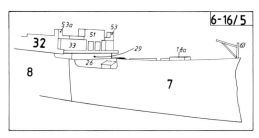

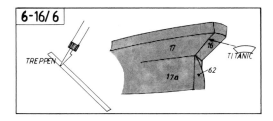

Step 7

Glue Part No. 33 forwards, between the Parts 30b and 32b just mounted, onto the already installed superstructure (Part 29). Part 33 must end flush with Part 29 in front. Part 33a is the superstructure; glue it on now. Glue Part 34 aft between Parts 30 and 32. Part 34 also rests on Part 28a at the position marked. Cut out Part 34a, score on the face and the reverse, and glue it in place.

NOTE: From here on, simplified versions of certain parts can be made, or smaller details omitted. This is described at the end of each step, as an alternative.

Step 8

Now install the upper decks, starting once again from the stern. Deck No. 35 fits exactly against Parts 30/32 at the rear (see diagram). Before inserting the decks, a strip of cardboard must be attached to each of the three deck sections as a tab to connect them. To install the three deck sections, Parts 35, 36 and 37, reach into the model from below.

NOTE: If you have not done so yet, you can now install the pre-assembled fixtures (windlasses, cargo hatches, etc.) on the well decks and the decks at bow and stern.

Glue Part 35a, the glasswork, onto deck No. 34 precisely in the middle, below the rearmost edge of deck No. 35 (see diagram).

Alternative: Part 35a can be either omitted entirely, or left without cutting out the windows.

Schritt 7

Bauteil 33 wird vorn zwischen die soeben aufgesetzten Teile 30b und 32b auf den bereits montierten Deckaufbau, (Teil 29) geklebt. Teil 33 muss mit Teil 29 vorn bündig abschließen. Bauteil 33a ist der Deckaufbau, er wird als Nächstes aufgeklebt. Bauteil 34 wird hinten zwischen die Teile 30 und 32 geklebt. Außerdem sitzt Teil 34 und Teil 28a an der gekennzeichneten Stelle. Bauteil 34a ausschneiden, vorder- und rückseitig ritzen, mit Klebstoff bestreichen und aufkleben.

ACHTUNG: Ab jetzt besteht die Möglichkeit, von einzelnen Teilen vereinfachte Versionen anzufertigen oder kleinere Details wegzulassen. Dazu wird am Ende eines jeden Arbeitsschrittes eine Alternative beschrieben.

Schritt 8

Nun werden die Oberdecks aufgesetzt. Auch hier fangen wir hinten an. Deck Nr. 35 schließt hinten bündig mit Teil 30/32 ab (siehe Skizze). Bevor die Decks eingepasst werden, muss zur Verbindung der drei Deckteile jeweils vorher ein Kartonstreifen als Verbindungslasche angebracht werden. Zur Montage aller drei Deckteile (35, 36, 37) greift man von unten in das Modell.

ANMERKUNG: Wer es bis jetzt noch nicht getan hat, kann die vorgefertigten Teile (Ankerwinden, Ladeluken etc.) auf Bug, Heck und die Welldecks montieren.

Die Verglasung 35a wird genau in die Mitte unter die hintere Kante von Deck 35 auf Deck 34 geklebt (s. Skizze).

Alternative: Man kann Teil 35a entweder ganz weglassen, oder man braucht die Fenster nicht auszuschneiden.

Étape 7

Coller l'élément 33 à l'avant entre les éléments 30b et 32b qui viennent d'être ajustés sur la superstructure du pont juste monté (élément 29).

L'élément 33 doit être ajusté très exactement à l'avant de l'élément 29. Coller alors l'élément 33a (superstructure du pont). Coller l'élément 34 à l'arrière entre les éléments 30 et 32. L'élément 34 repose, quant à lui, sur l'élément 28a à l'emplacement indiqué. Découper l'élément 34a, l'inciser des deux côtés et le coller.

ATTENTION : Dès lors, il est possible de réaliser des versions plus simples de divers éléments ou de laisser tomber de petits détails. Une alternative sera donc décrite à la fin de chaque étape.

Étape 8

Poser maintenant les ponts supérieurs. Commencer ici par la partie arrière. Le pont 35 est posé exactement contre l'élément 30/32. Avant d'ajuster les ponts, placer une bande de carton comme languette de liaison entre les trois parties du pont. Pour monter celles-ci (éléments 35, 36, 37), accéder à la maquette par le fond.

REMARQUE : Si ce n'est pas encore fait, on peut alors fixer les éléments préfabriqués (cabestans, écoutilles de chargement, etc.) sur la proue, la poupe et les ponts de lames.

Coller le vitrage 35a juste au milieu, sous la jointure arrière du pont 35 et contre le pont 34 (voir le croquis).

Alternative : On peut omettre les éléments 35a ou se passer de découper le vitrage.

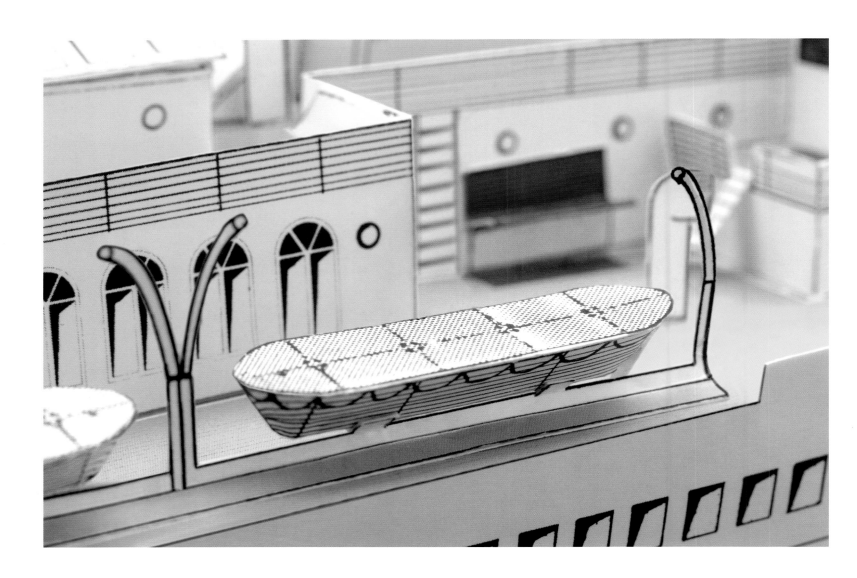

Step 9

Now begin with the superstructures on the main deck, starting from the rear again. Cut out Parts 38, 38a, and 38b, score them, and glue to the positions indicated. Mount Parts 39 and 39a on the rear of 38; fold 39b and 39c at right angles, and glue them also to 38.

Cut out Parts 40, 40a, and 40b, and score them; then glue walls 40 and 40a to the deck first. The top of the deck should be fitted and glued in place after the side walls have been installed. The same applies to all the remaining superstructures. First glue the walls precisely along the dot-and-dash line with the corresponding reference number, and only then glue in the corresponding decking.

Step 10

Cut out Parts 41 and 41a, score them, and glue to the position indicated. Cut out and glue on Parts 42 and 42a (light shaft for stairwell in first-class section) in the usual way. Cut out, score, and glue on Parts 43, 43a, and 43b. Cut out Parts 44 and 44a, score on front and reverse, and glue on as explained above.

Glue Parts 45 and 45a to the left and right of Part 44. Fit and glue in deck No. 45b like the others. Parts 46 and 46a look like a lifeguard's tower when assembled, but these are actually a compass.

Install superstructures 47–47b, light shaft 48–48a (also for a first-class stairwell), superstructure 49–49b, and the bridge, Part 50, as above.

Step 11

Adding Part 51 to the front of the bridge completes the deck erections. Now the first detail work begins. Glue Parts 52 and 52a to the dot-and-dash line forward on the upper deck. Glue the wing shelters at the wings, Parts 53–53c, along the dot-and-dash line. Assemble the navigation bridge at the stern, Parts 54–54e, and glue it to the previously installed supports, 54a–54d. Part 54e should be glued directly onto the railing from inside.

Step 12

Now cut out the davits, Parts 55–58. If you want to build all the boats separately, you must cut out the boats drawn on the piece, so that only the actual boat davits remain. The lower lines marked for scoring should be scored on the reverse, so that the printed side faces up. Now glue the empty davits to the positions indicated on the upper deck. After gluing on all four rows of davits, you can put together the individual boats. Curl the ends of the boats (Part 62), fold them lengthwise, and put on the boat covers (Part 61a). Then glue each assembled boat to two davits with extra-strength glue.

NOTE: Before gluing the boat covers, 61a, to the boat hulls, 61, pierce the ends of these parts with a needle and draw a piece of thread about 6 cm (2 3/8 in.) long through them, so that its ends emerge on the printed side. After assembly, fasten the ends to the davits.

Alternative: As you will have seen, it is not essential to cut out the boats printed on the boat davits. Leave the davits as printed, score them as described, and glue them in place. Thus you can spare yourself the work of building the boats, and the tricky cutting out of the individual davits.

Schritt 9

Wir beginnen nun mit den Aufbauten auf dem Hauptdeck. Auch hier fangen wir von hinten an. Die Bauteile 38, 38a, 38b ausschneiden, ritzen und auf die bezeichnete Stelle kleben. Die Bauteile 39 und 39a kommen an die Rückseite von 38; 39b und 39c werden rechtwinklig geknickt und ebenfalls an 38 geklebt.

Die Bauteile 40, 40a, 40b ausschneiden und ritzen; danach werden zuerst die Wände 40 und 40a auf das Deck geklebt. Das Deckdach wird erst nach der Montage der Seitenwände eingepasst und festgeklebt. Dies gilt auch für alle weiteren Deckaufbauten. Zuerst werden die Wände genau auf die strichpunktierte Linie mit den dazugehörigen Referenznummern geklebt – erst dann werden die entsprechenden Dächer eingeklebt.

Schritt 10

Die Bauteile 41 und 41a ausschneiden, ritzen und auf die bezeichnete Stelle kleben. Die Bauteile 42 und 42a (Lichtschacht für Treppenhaus der 1. Klasse) wie gehabt verarbeiten und aufkleben; Die Bauteile 43, 43a, 43b ausschneiden, ritzen und aufkleben. Die Bauteile 44 und 44a ausschneiden, vorder- und rückseitig ritzen und wie oben besprochen aufkleben.

Die Bauteile 45 und 45a werden links und rechts von Bauteil 44 aufgeklebt. Deck Nr. 45b einpassen und einkleben. Die Bauteile 46 und 46a sehen zusammengebaut aus wie ein Bademeisteraussichtsturm, sind aber in Wirklichkeit ein Kompass.

Die Deckaufbauten 47 bis 47b, der Lichtschacht für ein Treppenhaus der ersten Klasse 48 und 48a, die Deckaufbauten 49 bis 49b sowie die Brücke, Teil 50, werden wie besprochen montiert.

Schritt 11

Mit dem Abschluss der Brücke (vorn, Bauteil 51) sind die Deckaufbauten im Groben fertig. Jetzt beginnen die ersten Verfeinerungsarbeiten. Die Bauteile 52 und 52a werden stumpf auf die strichpunktierte Linie vorn auf dem Oberdeck geklebt. Die Nocks auf dem Seitenflügel 53 bis 53c werden entlang der strichpunktierten Linie aufgeklebt. Die Steuerbrücke, 54 bis 54e, am Heck wird fertiggestellt und auf die vorher angebrachten Stützen 54a bis 54d angeklebt. 54e wird direkt von innen an die Reling geklebt.

Schritt 12

Nun werden die Davits (Bauteile 55 bis 58) ausgeschnitten. Wer alle Boote einzeln bauen will, muss die aufgezeichneten Boote so ausschneiden, dass die Bootskräne frei dastehen. Die unteren Ritzlinien werden rückseitig geritzt, so dass die bedruckte Seite nach oben schaut. Nun werden die leeren Davits mit Klebstoff bestrichen und an die bezeichneten Stellen auf dem Oberdeck geklebt. Nachdem alle vier Davit-Reihen aufgeklebt wurden, können die einzelnen Boote hergestellt werden. Man rundet dazu die Enden der Boote, Bauteil 61, knickt sie der Länge nach und setzt die Bootsplane 61a auf. Dann wird das fertiggestellte Boot auf die jeweils zwei Nocken pro Davit stumpf mit Hartkleber aufgeklebt.

ACHTUNG: Bevor die Bootsplane 61a auf den Bootskörper 61 geklebt wird, sollten die Enden dieser Teile mit einer Nadel durchstochen und ein Faden von etwa 6 cm Länge durchgezogen werden. Die beiden Fadenenden, die zur bedruckten Seite hin vorn und hinten aus der Plane heraustreten, werden später, nach der Montage, mit den Davits verbunden.

Alternative: Es ist, wie sicher schon bemerkt, nicht notwendig, die aufgedruckten Boote auszuschneiden. Man belässt die Davits in dem gezeichneten Zustand, ritzt sie genau wie vorgesehen und klebt sie auf. Dadurch erspart man sich den Bau der Boote und das diffizile Ausschneiden der einzelnen Davits.

Étape 9

Commençons maintenant à monter les superstructures sur le pont principal. Ici aussi, nous débutons à l'arrière. Découper, inciser et coller à l'emplacement indiqué les éléments 38, 38a, 38b. Les éléments 39 et 39a sont fixés au dos de 38. Plier 39b et 39c et les coller également sur l'élément 38. Découper et inciser les éléments 40, 40a, 40b, puis coller d'abord les parois 40 et 40a sur le pont. N'ajuster et ne coller la couverture du pont qu'après avoir monté les parois latérales. Ceci vaut également pour toutes les autres superstructures du pont. Coller d'abord les parois sur la ligne interrompue en tenant compte des numéros de relation, et ensuite seulement les toitures correspondantes.

Étape 10

Découper, inciser et coller à l'emplacement indiqué les pièces 41 et 41a. Préparer de la même façon les éléments 42 et 42a (ouverture de la cage d'escalier de la première classe) et les coller.

Découper, inciser et coller les éléments 43, 43a, 43b. Découper les éléments 44 et 44a, les inciser de chaque côté et les coller en suivant les indications notées plus haut. Coller les éléments 45 et 45a à gauche et à droite de l'élément 44. Introduire et coller le pont 45a comme nous l'avons vu. Une fois montés, les éléments 46 et 46a ressemblent au siège surélevé d'un surveillant de baignade, mais en réalité il s'agit d'une boussole.

Monter selon les règles données les superstructures du pont (éléments 47–47b) ainsi que l'ouverture (éléments 48, 48a, également pour la cage d'escalier de la première classe), la superstructure du pont (éléments 49–49b) et la passerelle (élément 50).

Étape 11

L'achèvement de la passerelle avant (élément 51) marque la fin des superstructures du pont. Dès lors commencent les premiers travaux de finition. Coller les éléments 52, 52a le plus exactement possible sur la ligne interrompue à l'avant du pont supérieur. Coller les cordages de vergue sur l'aile (53–53c) en suivant la ligne interrompue. Monter la passerelle de commandement (54–54e) sur la poupe et la fixer sur les supports placés auparavant (54a–54d). De l'intérieur, coller directement l'élément 54e contre le bastingage.

Étape 12

Découper les bossoirs (éléments 55–58). Pour construire les canots un à un, les découper suivant le dessin de leurs contours de sorte que seules les grues des canots restent. Inciser au dos en suivant les lignes inférieures, de sorte que le côté imprimé soit en haut. Coller ensuite les bossoirs sur le pont aux emplacements indiqués. Une fois les quatre rangées de bossoirs collées, on peut passer au montage des canots. Pour ce, il faut arrondir leurs extrémités (élément 61), les plier dans le sens de la longueur et les couvrir de leur bâche (élément 61a). Coller les canots ainsi confectionnés bord à bord, sur les deux vergues de chaque bossoir, avec de la colle extra-forte.

ATTENTION : Avant de coller la bâche (61a) sur chaque canot, il conviendrait de percer les extrémités de ces éléments avec une aiguille et de tendre un fil d'environ 6 cm de long entre celles-ci. Plus tard, après le montage, relier aux bossoirs les deux extrémités du fil qui dépassent à l'avant et à l'arrière du côté imprimé.

Alternative : Comme vous l'avez sûrement remarqué, il n'est pas indispensable de découper les canots dessinés. Laisser alors les bossoirs comme ils sont, les inciser comme prévu et les coller. On évite ainsi la construction des canots et le découpage fastidieux de chaque bossoir.

Step 13

Parts 59 and 60 are two mast supports. Insert them from below into the holes already cut in the forward deck (18) and the 'tween deck (28a), and glue them in place from within. Glue the masts, Parts 59a and 60a, together, and slide them onto their mast supports.

Part 62 is the rudder of the giant liner. Glue the part on the reverse, then cut it out carefully, and fit it into the stern of the ship, as shown in the diagram. Slit the rear edge of the ship with the model-builder's knife at the height of the two tabs to be inserted, and insert the rudder. Now the tabs can be glued down from inside. Handle the anchor crane, Part 63, in the same way. After cutting it out carefully, glue it into the part of the forward deck (18) nearest the bows.

Alternative: The anchor crane does not have to be cut out completely. It is enough to cut it out along the outer profile.

Step 14

Now add all the ventilator cowls, shafts, etc., which led down into the lower decks of the *Titanic* (not in this model, of course), to the engine and boiler rooms. There the engineers, stokers, electricians and other engine-room crew worked on until the bitter end, so that there would still be power for broadcasting SOS signals, and also to prevent panic breaking out while the passengers and crew took to the lifeboats. For this reason, the ship remained brightly lit until it sank.

There are a total of 25 ventilator pipes, Part 65 – five on each segment. First glue the individual segments together on the reverse, and then cut them out carefully. Fasten them to the short dot-and-dash lines, ca. 5 mm (¼ inch) long, to be found on all the decks. Glue Parts 65a to the three circular areas. Assemble the Parts No. 67, of which there are five, into triangular ventilation grids, and glue them onto where they belong Glue the box-shaped ventilator shafts (seven parts), to the seven little white areas of the same shape.

Parts No. 69 are the benches, of which there are 37; glue them all to the brown rectangular areas on all decks. The Parts 69 are grouped into several blocks, arranged in rows to make it easier to work on them. Thus several benches can be scored at one time. (In this case, the piece is scored first, and then cut out.)

Alternative: All the ventilator pipes (Part 65) can be omitted, as can the rectangular ventilator shafts. This is why no reference numbers have been printed on the corresponding white areas on the decks. Keep the unused parts; you can always add them later, if you become more skilled and have time. The benches (Part 69) can also be omitted; the areas on which these benches would be mounted are coloured appropriately.

Step 15

Parts 66, 66a, 66b, and 66c: the eight cargo cranes of the *Titanic*. Assemble them as shown in the diagram, and glue to one another at the points indicated on the decks, at an angle of about 30°.

Alternative: The cargo cranes can also be made in a much simpler version, by gluing the Parts 64 together on the reverse, and then cutting them out carefully.

Schritt 13

Die Bauteile 59 und 60 sind zwei Mastfüße. Sie werden von unten in die bereits vorher eingeschnittenen Löcher im Bugdeck (18) und im Zwischendeck (28a) eingeführt und von innen festgeklebt.

Die Masten (59a und 60a) werden zusammengeklebt, und jeder wird auf seinen Mastfuß geschoben.

Bauteil 62 ist das Ruder unseres Giganten. Das Teil wird rückseitig verklebt, genau ausgeschnitten und dann (wie die Skizze zeigt) in das Heck des Schiffes eingepasst. Man schlitzt dazu in Höhe der beiden Einstecklaschen mit dem Bastelmesser die hintere Schiffskante und steckt das Ruder ein. Von innen kann man nun die Laschen festkleben. Der Ankerkran, Bauteil 63, wird genauso verarbeitet. Nach dem genauen Ausschneiden wird er in den vorderen Teil des Bugdecks (18) eingeklebt.

Alternative: Der Ankerkran muss nicht unbedingt ganz ausgeschnitten werden. Es reicht durchaus, nur die äußeren Konturen auszuschneiden.

Schritt 14

Nun werden alle Belüftungsrohre, Luftschächte und Belüftungskästen, die tief in den Bauch der *Titanic* zu den Maschinen- und Kesselräumen führten, montiert. In den Betriebsräumen arbeiteten die Maschinisten, Ingenieure, Heizer und Techniker bis zum bitteren Untergang, damit noch genug Strom zur Verfügung stand, um SOS zu funken; nicht zuletzt auch, um bei den Rettungsversuchen keine Panik ausbrechen zulassen. Aus diesem Grund war das Schiff bis zum Schluss hell erleuchtet.

Das Bauteil 65 (Belüftungsrohre) ist insgesamt 25 Mal in jedem Block vorhanden. Die einzelnen Blöcke werden erst rückseitig verklebt und dann genau ausgeschnitten. Sie werden auf die kleinen ca. 5 mm langen strichpunktierten Linien auf allen Decks verteilt.

Die Bauteile mit der Nummer 65a werden auf die drei kreisrunden Flächen geklebt. Die Bauteile mit der Nummer 67 werden zu dreieckigen Belüftungsgittern geformt und an die entsprechenden Stellen geklebt. Von ihnen gibt es fünf Stück. Die sieben Bauteile mit der Nummer 68, die kastenförmigen Luftschächte, werden auf die sieben kleinen weißen Flächen gleichen Formats geklebt. Vom Bauteil 69 (Sitzbänke) gibt es 37 Stück, die alle auf die braunen rechteckigen Flächen auf allen Decks geklebt werden. Die Bauteile 69 sind in mehreren Blöcken angeordnet, die zur leichteren Verarbeitung alle in einer Reihe angelegt wurden. Dadurch kann man mit einem Ritzen mehrere Bänke gleichzeitig fertigstellen. (Merke: In diesem Fall erst ritzen, dann ausschneiden.)

Alternative: Alle Belüftungsrohre (Bauteil 65) können weggelassen werden, ebenso können die rechteckigen Luftschächte weggelassen werden. Deshalb wurde auf den entsprechenden weißen Flächen auf den Decks keine, in diesem Fall störende Referenznummer angebracht. Man sollte die nicht verbastelten Teile aufheben, und wenn man Lust und Zeit und die inzwischen erworbene Fingerfertigkeit hat nachträglich aufsetzen.

Die Sitzbänke 69 können ebenfalls weggelassen werden; die Flächen, auf denen diese Bänke stehen würden, sind in entsprechender Farbe gedruckt.

Schritt 15

Die Bauteile 66, 66a, 66b und 66c sind die acht Ladekräne der *Titanic*. Sie werden, wie die Skizze zeigt, zusammengesetzt und auf die bezeichneten Stellen auf den Decks in einem Winkel von ca. 30° zueinander geklebt.

Alternative: Die Ladekräne können auch ganz entschieden vereinfacht werden, wenn man die Bauteile mit der Nummer 64 zuerst rückseitig verklebt und dann genau ausschneidet.

Étape 13

Les éléments 59 et 60 sont deux pieds de mât. Les introduire par-dessous dans les trous prévus à cet effet sur le pont avant (élément 18) et sur l'entrepont, puis, les coller de l'intérieur. Coller les mâts 59a et 60a et poser chacun sur son pied.

L'élément 62 représente le gouvernail du géant des mers. Coller le dos de l'élément, le découper avec soin, puis l'insérer sur la poupe du navire (voir le croquis). Procéder en incisant, avec un cutter de modélisme, le bord arrière du navire à la hauteur des deux languettes de fixation, et y placer le gouvernail. Dès lors, on peut coller les languettes de l'intérieur. Procéder de même pour la grue de l'ancre (élément 63). Après l'avoir découpée soigneusement, la coller dans la partie avant du pont avant (élément 18).

Alternative : Il n'est pas absolument nécessaire de découper cette grue dans tous ses détails. Le découpage des contours extérieurs s'avère suffisant.

Étape 14

Maintenant commence le montage de tous les tuyaux de ventilation, des bouches et des installations d'aération qui conduisent, dans les entrailles du *Titanic*, aux salles des machines et des chaudières (pas dans cette maquette, bien sûr !). Là, les machinistes, ingénieurs, chauffeurs et techniciens travaillèrent jusqu'à la submersion du navire pour assurer la production d'électricité et lancer des SOS. C'est la raison pour laquelle l'éclairage fonctionna jusqu'au bout sur le navire. On évita ainsi une panique pendant les tentatives de sauvetage.

Il existe au total vingt-cinq tuyaux d'aération (élément 65), cinq par bloc. Coller d'abord chaque bloc au dos, puis les découper minutieusement. Les répartir sur les petites lignes interrompues d'environ 5 mm de longueur sur tous les ponts. Coller l'élément 65a sur les trois surfaces rondes. Modeler les éléments 67 en forme de grilles d'aération triangulaires et les coller aux emplacements correspondants. Elles sont au nombre de cinq. Coller les éléments 68 (bouches d'aération en forme de boîte, au nombre de sept), sur les sept petites surfaces blanches de même format.

Éléments 69 (bancs) : Coller les trente-sept exemplaires sur les surfaces rectangulaires marron se trouvant sur chaque pont. Ces éléments sont classés en plusieurs blocs placés sur une même rangée afin de faciliter le façonnage. Ainsi, d'un seul coup de cutter, on peut réaliser plusieurs bancs. (Remarque : Dans ce cas, inciser d'abord et découper ensuite.)

Alternative : On peut se passer de tous les tuyaux d'aération (65), de même que des bouches d'aération. Pour cette raison, on a renoncé à noter les numéros de référence, gênants dans ce cas, sur les surfaces blanches correspondantes sur les ponts. On peut conserver les éléments non utilisés pour les ajouter plus tard, quand on en aura le temps ou l'envie, ou qu'on aura acquis une certaine dextérité. On peut aussi se passer des bancs (éléments 69). Les surfaces où ils devraient être placés sont imprimées de la couleur appropriée.

Étape 15

Éléments 66, 66a, 66b et 66c : les huit grues de chargement du *Titanic*. Les monter conformément au croquis et les coller aux emplacements indiqués sur les ponts. Elles doivent conserver un angle de 30° environ les unes par rapport aux autres.

Alternative : On peut simplifier les grues de chargement. Il suffit de coller les éléments 64 au dos et de ne les découper qu'après.

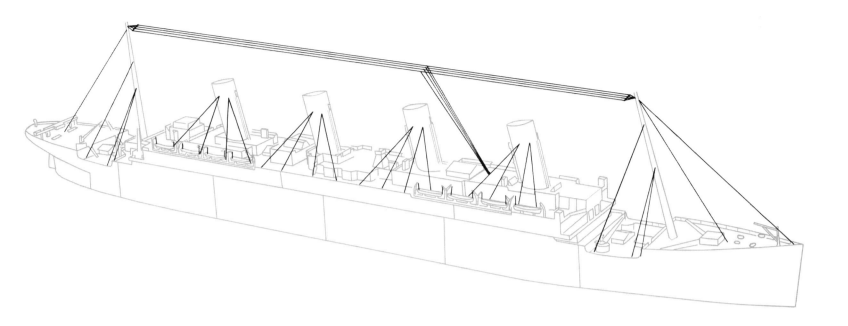

Step 16

Now, to crown the model, the funnels! It may interest you to know that only three of the four funnels actually functioned as smokestacks. The fourth was merely a dummy. Since the three funnels (Parts 70–70f) are assembled in the same way as the fourth (Parts 71–71f), only Part 70 is explained.

First cut out Part 70, and curl it on your thigh as described above. Glue Part 70a onto the funnel from within, just under the uppermost edge. Glue Part 70b together on the reverse, and cut it out. Then brush glue onto the edges of the oval, and wind the funnel around the oval, immediately below the black strip 70a. Now glue the steam whistles and pressure relief valves, Parts 70c–70e, to the funnel. Part 70f (also glued together on the reverse) is should be glued to the bottom edge of the funnel for added stability.

Rigging

Your *Titanic* will look even better if you string threads to represent the stays and shrouds. This takes much patience, but is a lot of fun, and does not take too much time once you have the hang of it. There are no set instructions for this; you must try for yourself, and see what method works best for you. I recommend actually sewing the threads. That is, poke holes carefully with a needle through the black dots in the decks and funnels. Then thread a large length of thread through the needle, and start threading from below through the deck into the mast or funnel, and back into the deck from above (be very careful that it does not get tangled). There is no need to do all the rigging with one piece of thread – it is a good idea to do it in several stages.

Where the rigging goes is shown in the drawings. That's it.

**There it is, big and beautiful,
and ready to sink – your S. S. *Titanic*!**

Schritt 16

Die Krönung sind die Schornsteine. Wissenswert ist vielleicht, dass von den vier Schornsteinen nur drei wirklich ihrer Funktion als Schornstein nachkamen. Der vierte war lediglich eine Attrappe. Da die drei echten Schornsteine (Bauteile 70 bis 70f mit der Attrappe (Bauteile 71 bis 71f identisch sind, wird hier nur Nr. 70 erklärt.

Zuerst wird Bauteil Nr. 70 ausgeschnitten und auf dem Oberschenkel gerundet. Bauteil 70a wird direkt unter die obere Kante von innen an den Schornstein geklebt. Bauteil 70b wird rückseitig verklebt und ausgeschnitten. Dann bestreicht man die Kanten des Ovals mit Klebstoff und „wickelt" den Kamin um das Oval herum, und zwar genau unter dem schwarzen Streifen 70a. Nun werden die Dampfpfeifen und Überdruckventile, Bauteile 70c–70e, an den Kamin geklebt. Zur Stabilisierung wird Bauteil 70f (ebenfalls rückseitig stumpf mit Klebstoff verklebt) an die untere Kante in den Kamin geklebt.

Vertäuung

Ihre *Titanic* sieht noch besser aus, wenn Sie sie mit Fäden bespannen. Dies ist eine wirkliche Geduldsarbeit, die allerdings großen Spaß macht. Wenn man erst einmal angefangen hat, geht es doch recht schnell. Für die Vertäuung gibt es keine Bauanleitung, jeder ist sein eigener Herr und Meister und muss selbst herausfinden, wie es am besten geht. Ich empfehle Ihnen allerdings, die Fäden regelrecht zu nähen. Stoßen Sie mit einer Nadel vorsichtig Löcher in die schwarzen Punkte in die Decks und in die Kamine. Nehmen Sie dann einen sehr langen Faden (dabei muss man gut aufpassen, dass er sich nicht verheddert), fangen Sie an einer Stelle an, den Faden (mit der Nadel) von unten durch das Deck in den Mast oder den Kamin und wieder von oben in das Deck zu ziehen. Man muss nicht gleich mit einem Faden alles bespannen – sinnvoll ist es, die Vertäuung in mehreren Etappen vorzunehmen.

Wohin welche Bespannung gehört, sehen Sie aus den Zeichnungen. Das war's.

**So, da steht sie nun, groß und schön
und bereit unterzugehen: Ihre *Titanic*.**

Étape 16

Le « fin du fin » : les cheminées. Il faut peut-être mentionner que seules trois des quatre cheminées assuraient leur fonction en tant que telles, la quatrième n'étant qu'un leurre. Les trois cheminées (élément 70–70f) étant identiques à l'élément 71–71f, l'explication ne porte que sur 70. Découper l'élément 70 et le façonner sur la cuisse conformément aux instructions de départ. Coller l'élément 70a de l'intérieur, contre la cheminée, au-dessus du bord supérieur. Coller l'élément 70b au dos et le découper. Puis badigeonner de colle les bords de l'ovale et « enrouler » véritablement la cheminée autour de l'ovale, juste au-dessous du trait noir 70a. Coller ensuite les sifflets à vapeur et les soupapes de surcompression (éléments 70c–70e) sur la cheminée. Coller l'élément 70f (collé également au dos) dans la cheminée sur le bord inférieur afin de la stabiliser.

Amarrage

Votre *Titanic* sera encore plus beau si vous le tendez de filins. C'est certes un travail de longue haleine, mais fort intéressant, et une fois commencé il est vite accompli. Pour le consolider, il n'existe pas de directives : chacun doit de son propre chef trouver la meilleure solution. Je vous conseille cependant de coudre en perçant prudemment les points noirs sur les ponts et les cheminées avec une aiguille. Prendre ensuite un fil très long (veiller à ce qu'il ne s'emmêle pas). Commencer à un certain endroit à passer l'aiguille enfilée du fond du pont à la cheminée, ou dans le mât, puis, du haut du navire au pont. Il n'est pas nécessaire d'accomplir ce travail avec un seul fil ; il est même plus sage de procéder en plusieurs étapes.

Les dessins vous montrent le parcours de chaque fil. C'est tout !

**Et voilà, votre *Titanic* apparaît dans toute
sa splendeur... et paré à sombrer.**

© 2012 TASCHEN GmbH
Hohenzollernring 53, D–50672 Köln, Germany
www.taschen.com

Drawings and instructions: Thomas Siwek
Editorial coordination: Simone Philippi, Cologne
Design: Sense/Net Art Direction, Andy Disl and Birgit Eichwede, Cologne. www.sense-net.net
Production coordination: Horst Neuzner, Tina Ciborowius, Cologne
English translation: Timothy Slater, Michael Hulse

Printed in China
ISBN 978-3-8365-3082-8